This book is dedicated to all who have served, those who now serve,
and those yet to serve in the United States Air Force.
Thank you, and may God bless you.

TO BE A U.S.
AIR FORCE PILOT

Henry M. Holden

First published in 2004 by MBI, an imprint of MBI Publishing Company, Galtier Plaza, Suite 200, 380 Jackson Street, St. Paul, MN 55101-3885 USA

MBI titles are also available at discounts in bulk quantity for industrial or sales-promotional use. For details write to Special Sales Manager at Motorbooks International Wholesalers & Distributors, Galtier Plaza, Suite 200, 380 Jackson Street, St. Paul, MN 55101-3885 USA.

Library of Congress Cataloging-in-Publication Data
Holden, Henry M.
     To be a U.S. Air Force Pilot / by Henry Holden.
         p. cm. — (To be a—)
     ISBN 0-7603-1791-7 (pbk. : alk. paper)
     1. Air pilots, Military—Training of—United States. 2. Air pilots, Military—Vocational guidance—United States. 3. United States. Air Force—Officers—Vocational guidance. I. Title. II. Series

UG638.H64 2004
623.74'6048—dc22

Edited by Steve Gansen
Designed by LeAnn Kuhlmann

On the front cover: A view from a cockpit shows F-16s in formation. These Fighting Falcons are from the 48th Fighter Wing at Luke Air Force Base, Arizona.

On the frontispiece: A close-up of a U.S. Air Force weapon systems officer in the cockpit of an F-16DJ Fighting Falcon during an air combat training mission.

On the title page: A pilot looks out from the cockpit of an F-16C Fighting Falcon during a combat air patrol mission over the Eastern Seaboard of the United States.

On the contents page: A close-up of an F-16 pilot.

On the back cover, top: An F-16 shoots an air-to-air missile. *Bottom:* In this cockpit shot, an F-16 pilot is "checking his six."

About the author: Henry M. Holden is the author of 11 adult books, 19 children's books, and more than 600 magazine articles on aviation history. In 1994 he received the New Jersey Institute of Technology's Author's Award, and that same year was mentioned in the Congressional Record for his works on women in aviation. Holden has been an aviation commentator for the History Channel, and lives in northwestern New Jersey.

Unless otherwise noted, all photographs are courtesy of the U.S. Air Force.

Printed in China

CONTENTS

Foreword

Henry Holden has rendered the public an invaluable service by presenting the best, most technically accurate, and supremely readable account of what it means to become a pilot in the United States Air Force. In a clear, concise, page-turning style, Holden tells us everything that anyone should know about becoming a pilot in the United States Air Force, including both the joys and the sorrows.

This book is extremely important today, when the demand for qualified pilots is high. The Air Force's equipment is more sophisticated than ever, and it will become even more exotic in the future. Pilots and crewmembers will have to be increasingly proficient at handling exotic aircraft, information systems, and weapons in the future.

Holden begins with the requirements for becoming an officer in the USAF, a prerequisite for anyone wishing to enter pilot training. This is the first in a series of demanding assessments that will continue throughout a pilot's career. Only the most highly qualified are accepted for officer training, and Holden points out the possible routes to the shiny golden bar of a second lieutenant. His description of entrance to, and life at, the beautiful United States Air Force Academy is excellent and will inspire young men and women to strive for admission.

In this cockpit shot, an F-16 pilot is "checking his six."

The profiles of typical students in the joint specialized undergraduate pilot training program are especially valuable for anyone contemplating becoming a pilot in the USAF, for they reveal just how stringent the selection criteria are. These students demonstrate that the pursuit of wings is serious business, unlike any representations from Hollywood films. From the day of application to the day that wings are pinned on, the prospective pilot is exercised to their full capabilities, and Holden gives insight into just how demanding the task of learning to fly really is.

Fortunately, Holden also portrays how rewarding the pursuit is and lets you see why young men and women are so eager to sacrifice so much of their time and effort for the goal. Besides academics and the thrill of the flightline, there are other challenging tasks, including enduring the black-out-inducing effects of a ride on a human centrifuge, learning the physiology of flight firsthand by training in an altitude chamber, and becoming familiar with the effects of spatial disorientation. The USAF investment in capital equipment for training is enormous, and is highlighted by complete sets of simulators, which can accurately duplicate every phase of flight. It is in these simulators that potential pilots learn their procedures and safely make their mistakes.

Holden is perhaps at his best in describing the rapid progress pilots make as the program progresses and the opportunity is given for solo flight, aerobatics, instrument flight, and formation flying. Throughout the training process, the student is carefully evaluated by his instructor and by others. This careful check on performance is a characteristic of military aviation, one that distinguishes it from many other professions. At least twice a year, but more often in practice, every pilot is given a thorough test of their abilities to fly the aircraft under every sort of condition. This continues throughout the career of every pilot. In addition, additional checks are given in simulators to cover conditions too dangerous to practice in actual flight. No gentleman's (or gentlewoman's) C grades

The C-130 Hercules has a number of specific uses. One of the AC-130H/U gunship missions is close air support of troops, convoy escort, and urban operations. The MC-130P Combat Shadow aircraft flies clandestine, or low-visibility, low-altitude, missions penetrating hostile territory. The C-130 has other missions as well, such as bug spraying and hurricane hunting. It is seen here dispensing countermeasures.

are given—you have to be good at every aspect of the test, or you are failed. After a failure, additional training is given, along with a recheck. Repeated failures are a ticket back to civilian life.

During flight training, a point is reached where decisions must be made about a student's future training. The student's flying and academic performance are considered, as well as their individual preferences, but the USAF will decide based on its assessment of the student and its current needs. These decisions will determine whether the student will become a fighter pilot or a bomber, transport, or tanker pilot.

One of the more engaging aspects of this book is the author's ability to put the reader in the cockpit. At intervals, Holden takes the reader along for a ride, describing the mission, using the standard radio procedures, and otherwise simulating the intricacies of a flight in a modern military aircraft.

The book should appeal to three large audiences. The first is high school graduates who are considering what they should do with their lives. Holden's accurate, fast-moving sketches of the joys and sorrows of becoming a flyer will help them decide. The second audience is college students, who participate in many extracurricular activities, but have not yet decided on how to best use their new skills. The third audience, and probably the largest and most surprising, is older generations of flyers who will be amazed by the close resemblance of today's young potential aces with those of the past. These veterans will be fascinated by the refinements in pilot training that Holden so aptly discusses.

Henry Holden takes the reader beyond undergraduate pilot training to the endless rewards of being a pilot— and the training that continues even after the coveted silver wings are won. I suspect that the prospect of these rewards will induce many young men and women to enter the United Stated Air Force to learn to fly.

—Colonel Walter J. Boyne, USAF (Ret.)

A KC-135 refuels a B-2A Spirit in the sunset. Tanker aircraft were ordered into Iraqi airspace to establish refueling "tracks" so strike fighters could remain on station over their "kill boxes" longer.

Preface

Amid countless books on the United States Air Force, this is the first to thoroughly cover how to become a U.S. Air Force pilot—from the first military haircut, to the coveted silver wings, to horizons far beyond.

Not everyone can succeed in Air Force pilot training. First, the pilot candidate must become a commissioned officer, a process that will weed out those lacking in leadership potential. Next is pilot training, where only the most highly motivated, focused, and determined candidates will survive the 52 weeks of intensive training. These young men and women endure hardships and satisfactions unknown in the civilian world. Why do they endure where others give up? Perhaps it's the challenge and the desire to build on the legacy of such innovators as General Billy Mitchell, an outspoken visionary for an independent air force who accurately predicted the attack on Pearl Harbor and the future of aerial warfare. Or perhaps they've been inspired by the courage of General Jimmy Doolittle and his men, whose daring raid on Japan gave America a much needed morale boost.

A P-47 Thunderbolt, *Tarheel Hal,* is followed by two demonstration-team F-16 Fighting Falcons. The P-47 Thunderbolt was one of the Army Air Force's front-line fighters during World War II.

This B-25 Mitchell bomber, part of a reenactment of Doolittle's Raid, takes off from the deck of the USS Ranger. On April 18, 1942, Lieutenant Colonel James "Jimmy" Doolittle commanded 16 B-25s launched from the aircraft carrier USS Hornet to bomb Japan. The raid inflicted little physical damage, but accomplished its intended mission, striking a stunning psychological blow against Japan. The Mitchell B-25 bomber was a sturdy World War II weapons platform. The twin-tail design made it solid and controllable, even with one of its two engines out.

Then there's pioneering aviator General Henry "Hap" Arnold, a vocal supporter of Mitchell's separate air force, who forged the Eighth Air Force into an aerial hammer that cleared the skies over Europe in preparation for the D-day landings. So effective was Allied air power that on D-day only two enemy fighters showed up over the beaches of Normandy. Mitchell's pre-World War II vision of a long-range bomber later materialized as the B-29 bomber. General Elwood Quesada was widely recognized as a tactical air expert during World War II. He used his Ninth Air Force to savage enemy ground forces. General Curtis LeMay, considered the father of the Strategic Air Command (SAC), took the piston-powered Air Force into the jet age and made SAC the world's foremost airpower. General William "Spike" Momyer, through a communications deception, began one of the most intensive air combat operations of the Vietnam War by drawing a reluctant North Vietnamese Air Force into combat. In one 15-minute period, American F-4s destroyed half of the North Vietnamese active air force's inventory. General Wilbur Creech, who started on the bottom rung of the military as a private, turned the Tactical Air Command into an organization whose achievements were so sweeping that its precision bombings during the first Gulf War were broadcast on worldwide television.

Today's demanding Air Force pilot training, advanced aircraft technology, and superior electronic weapons give the United States Air Force a unique advantage. Like their predecessors, current Air Force leadership understands the imperative of owning the skies.

This U.S. Air Force F-16 Fighting Falcon pilot, whose call sign is "Vixen," gives the thumbs up signal from the cockpit of her aircraft as she prepares for a mission in support of Operation Iraqi Freedom.

Acknowledgments

Writing this book has been both a great privilege and pleasure. The privilege has come from meeting and talking with some of the best pilots in the world, and from listening to their training stories and adventures. The pleasure has come from being able to share this with others. I am indebted to many people who helped make this book possible. Without the enthusiasm and assistance of the "insiders"—the men and women of the United States Air Force, who gave of their time, knowledge, and counsel, and some of whom wish to remain in the background—this book would not have been possible.

Captain Chad Robbins, F-15E Strike Eagle driver and instructor pilot, spent several hours with me discussing not only his personal experiences, but guiding me through some of the inner workings and nuances of training Air Force pilots. Captain Robbins read the manuscript, and his comments were invaluable to my presenting an accurate picture of Air Force pilots and their training.

My special thanks to Colonel Walter J. Boyne, USAF (Ret.), for providing the foreword. Colonel Boyne, a pilot with over 5,000 hours, is a former director of the National Air and Space Museum and the author of more than 30 books and over 400 magazine articles on aviation. He also appears on, and serves as a consultant to, various cable television shows dedicated to aviation. Over the years, Walt has remained a friend and supporter of my writing endeavors.

It was a pleasure to work with my editor, Steve Gansen, who listened to and answered my hundreds of questions with patience and professionalism.

Lieutenant Colonel Phillip J. Beaudoin, USAF, Commander, 557th Flying Training Squadron, USAFA, provided much valuable information on the Air Force Academy's airmanship programs, and Major Brandon Baker, USAF, Assistant Director of Operations 94th FTS, USAFA, read the manuscript.

Other valuable input came from Captain Sean M. Cotter, Executive Officer, USAF Air Demonstration Squadron, Thunderbird #10; Major Darin Defendorf, USAF, Director of Operations, 98th FTS, USAFA; Major Mark Matticola, USAF, Assistant Director of Operations, 94th FTS, USAFA; Second Lieutenant Rob Arnett, USAF; and Major Anne Fletcher, USAF (Ret.).

John VanWinkle of the USAFA Public Affairs Office provided academy contacts and some great photographs. William T. Y'Blood, Chief, Reference Branch, Air Force History, provided information on Medal of Honor pilots. Correspondence from Ed Fitzgerald, whose daughter Sharon graduated in the class of 2001, and Jim Mumaw, whose daughter will soon graduate, were also helpful.

Of course, none of this would have been possible without the support and encouragement of my wife, Nancy. She took the time to read the manuscript and provide important suggestions. My son Steve read the manuscript for style and provided me with valuable input and suggestions. To everyone, my thanks.

A B-2 approaches a refueling boom. During Operation Iraqi Freedom, the Air Force conducted its first-ever joint B-1, B-2, and B-52 operation with all three bomber types in one strike package employing GPS-guided weapons to generate a devastating attack on a single target.

ONE

Becoming an Officer

All U.S. Air Force pilot candidates must first become commissioned officers. Those selected for pilot training enter from one of several sources: civilian colleges and universities through Air Force Reserve Officer Training Corps (ROTC), the Air Force Academy, or Officer Training School (OTS) if the candidate already has a college degree.

Reserve Officer Training Corps (ROTC)

ROTC is a government program that offers scholarships to college students to provide money for tuition, books, fees, and a monthly living allowance. ROTC introduces cadets to the inner workings of the Air Force, and offers them an opportunity to develop leadership skills. ROTC detachments will visit bases to observe Air Force operations and gain exposure to a variety of Air Force missions and the broad range of officer career fields. As one cadet from North Carolina A&T State University explained, "I left Shaw Air Force Base that day without a doubt in my mind that I knew exactly what I wanted to do in life; fly with the best planes, and the greatest air force in the world!"

A first-class cadet inspects trainees upon their arrival at Basic Cadet Training.

13

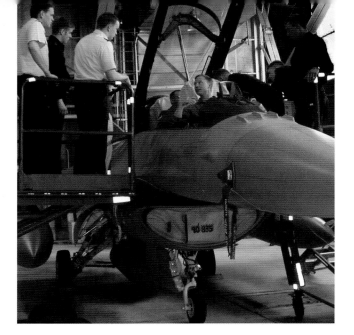

Air Force ROTC cadets are students who attend regular colleges and lead normal college lives. They do not wear a uniform every day, but only to ROTC classes and occasional special events. ROTC cadets attend a weekly leadership laboratory where they study Air Force customs, courtesies, drill, and ceremonies. The rest of the time, ROTC cadets dress and look like any other college student.

Left: Members of the Brigham Young University AFROTC Detachment 855 visit Edwards Air Force Base to get a close-up look at the Air Force flight-test mission.

Below: Cadet squadrons are marching.

ROTC students must maintain a minimum grade point average of 2.0 on a 4.0 scale. They must also receive a waiver for any civil infractions, such as speeding tickets and other minor violations. Students must be commissioned before reaching their 29th birthday, and must take the Air Force Officer Qualifying Test (AFOQT). The test measures aptitudes used to select candidates for officer commissioning programs, including the flight-training program. The AFOQT consists of 16 subtests and takes four-and-a-half hours to complete.

All potential officers must pass a battery of physical, psychological, and background tests. An FBI background check is conducted, and citizenship is verified. Any deviant behaviors, financial irresponsibility, or membership in organizations whose intent is to overthrow the United States government are grounds for automatic rejection.

An individual does not need to be an athlete in order to pass the ROTC physical fitness requirements. Some effort and preparation, however, are required. Most individuals in good physical health should pass the tests if they have a regular program of aerobic (fitness- building) and anaerobic (strength-building) exercises as part of their lifestyle.

The comprehensive physical exam includes a clinical interview and lab work, including screening for HIV, chemical or drug use, and abnormal blood chemistry. Students must not have a history of hay fever, asthma, or allergies after age 12, must meet Air Force weight and physical conditioning requirements, and must have a standing height of 64 to 77 inches and a sitting height of 34 to 40 inches. Students must have normal color vision, with distance vision uncorrected to 20/70 and near vision uncorrected to 20/20, and must meet refraction, accommodation, and astigmatism requirements. Prior corrective eye surgery may be a disqualifier. If students are medically qualified and desire a flying career, they must compete for pilot allocations about 15 months before graduation and commissioning.

ROTC cadets wishing to become pilots must take a Class 1 flight physical, the same test required for a civilian private pilot certificate (PPC). They must complete an introductory flight training (IFT) program, which was developed to lower attrition rates at joint specialized undergraduate pilot training (JSUPT), the Air Force-administered flight-training program where Air Force, Navy, and Marine officers become qualified as military aviators. The IFT program has two requirements: complete 50 hours of flying (including solo time) and earn a PPC. After graduating from college and completing all ROTC requirements, students are commissioned as second lieutenants and compete for pilot-candidate slots with the other ROTC graduates at large.

In 2003, 18.8 percent of Air Force officers were commissioned through the Air Force Academy, 41.5 percent through the Reserve Officer Training Corps, and 21.9 percent through Officer Training School. The remaining 17.8 percent were commissioned from other sources, including direct appointment.

ROTC PHYSICAL FITNESS TEST (PFT)
Cadets enrolled in ROTC take the physical fitness test every fall and spring semester. The PFT is comprised of three events in the order listed below, and scores are determined by age and gender. All events must be completed, a short rest period is allowed between events, and there is no minimum passing score. As long as students achieve the minimum passing standard for each of the three events, they pass the PFT.

REPETITIONS

AGE	MALE	FEMALE
SIT-UPS (IN 2 MINUTES, FOLLOWED BY A 2-MINUTE REST)		
Up to 24	53	53
25-29	50	50
30-34	42	42
PUSH-UPS (IN 2 MINUTES, FOLLOWED BY A 2-MINUTE REST)		
Up to 24	42	19
25-29	40	17
30-34	36	15
1.5-MILE RUN		
Up to 24	12:00	14.30
25-29	12:30	15.00
30+	13:00	15.30

OFFICER TRAINING SCHOOL

Officer Training School, located at Maxwell Air Force Base in Alabama and Lackland Air Force Base in Texas, is another form of basic officer training. OTS is a route toward becoming an Air Force officer for college graduates who did not belong to ROTC, or for enlisted Air Force personnel graduating from college. As a group, OTS pilot applicants tend to be older than other pilot applicants, and may have significant civilian flying experience. Many have prior military experience, typically as active duty enlisted personnel.

Enlisted Air Force members applying to OTS compete at large with civilians. Competition is stiff, but statistics show that enlisted members have an edge over civilian applicants. The selection rate is about 25 to 30 percent for enlisted applicants, and about 10 percent less for civilians. Applicants must have a bachelor's degree, or be within 270 days of completing one and must pass the AFOQT. The average OTS student is 28 years old and has a grade-point average of 3.23.

"This is a tough school," said one graduate. "You have to want it 110 percent, and be ready for the long haul." The intensive 12-week program includes classroom work, lectures, and exercises to develop leadership, team-building, and officer skills. For civilians, it is like walking into basic training, and many candidates are unprepared for the physical pace and strict regimentation.

UNITED STATES AIR FORCE ACADEMY

Soon after creation of the Air Force in 1947, a board of civilian and military educators met to plan a curriculum for an academy that would meet the needs of the new Air Force. The board determined that Air Force requirements could not be met by simply expanding the other service academies, and recommended the establishment of an Air Force Academy. In 1954, President Dwight D. Eisenhower signed a law authorizing the creation of the United States Air Force Academy (USAFA) in Colorado Springs, Colorado. The first class of 306 men began training at temporary facilities at Denver's Lowry Air Force Base on July 11, 1955. The cadets moved to the permanent location three years later, where 207 second lieutenants graduated in 1959.

In a debate about whether pilot training should be provided at the Academy, one side argued that flying was an intrinsic part of an Air Force officer's career. The other side argued that the Academy should be an institution of higher learning like West Point, the Coast Guard Academy, and the Naval Academy. The initial plan called for giving all cadets pilot training in their third and fourth years. Those unable to complete that training would receive additional training to prepare for non-rated careers. (Rated officers are those officers who have earned Pilot Wings, Navigator Wings, Air Battle Manager Wings—officers that direct operations on either AWACS or JSTARS—or a Missileer's Badge. All other officers are considered non-rated.) A compromise was eventually reached—flight theory and training were integrated into the academic program, along with a minimum of actual flight instruction.

Other factors enlivened the debate. One was the location of the Academy in the Colorado mountains. The proposed site was over 7,000 feet above sea level, and opponents feared the treacherous air currents, the mountainous terrain, the adverse effects of the thinner air on takeoff and approach, and the high altitude on small training airplanes' engine performance. The arguments became moot when Charles Lindbergh flew a small plane over the site and declared the area suitable for flight training.

Cadet flight training was originally conducted at Peterson Air Force Base, about 12 miles from the Academy. In 1965, the secretary of defense authorized the construction of an airstrip near the south entrance of the Academy. A small airstrip was easier to fund through Congress than a large airfield.

Although more officers are commissioned through ROTC each year, the odds of becoming a pilot through the Air Force Academy are much better than through the ROTC/OTS routes. The Academy has graduated about 36,000 cadets; 24,500 were pilot-qualified at graduation,

On August 1, 1907, the U.S. Army Signal Corps established an Aeronautical Division to "take charge of all matters pertaining to military ballooning, air machines, and all kindred subjects." The National Security Act of 1947 authorized the creation of a separate U.S. Air Force. Although President Harry S. Truman signed the act on July 26, 1947, the Air Force's official birthday is September 18, 1947, the day the first secretary of the Air Force, Stewart Symington, was sworn in.

and 20,500 of those have gone on to pilot training. On average, at least half of Air Force Academy graduates qualify for pilot training. Depending on the needs of the Air Force, pilot slots vary from year to year, but have been averaging about 1,000 a year. Both the ROTC and the Academy receive the same number of pilot-slot allocations. The Academy gets 45 percent (554 slots in 2003), and ROTC receives an equal percentage. OTS gets about 8 percent, and the remaining 2 percent go to other special programs, such as merchant marine officers. In the Academy's Class of 2003, of the 974 graduates, 554 went to JSUPT, contrasted with the thousands of ROTC graduates competing for the ROTC's 554 slots.

APPOINTMENT

Being appointed and accepted to the Air Force Academy is the most difficult, competitive, and rewarding route to becoming an Air Force officer and pilot. About 13 percent of all applicants are accepted.

Only the brightest, most physically fit, and most highly motivated young men and women are admitted to the Academy. On July 1 of the year of application, candidates must be at least 17 (but less than 23) years old, have no dependents, have good moral character, and be unmarried. Students are typically 18-year-old high school graduates, although older students, particularly those those who are already enlisted, are also admitted. Some come from non-credit prep schools, and applicants come from all 50 states and 10 foreign countries.

All Academy applicants must pass a battery of physical, psychological, and background tests. An FBI background check is completed, citizenship is verified, and any deviant behaviors, financial irresponsibility, or membership in organizations whose intent is to overthrow the United States government are grounds for automatic rejection.

The Academy gives all applicants a comprehensive physical exam, including an EKG, a clinical interview, and lab work. Screening is done for HIV, past or present chemical or drug dependency, and any abnormal blood chemistry. In addition, height, weight, body fat, hearing, vision, orthopedic, and neurological screening are necessary to ensure the applicants meet the physical challenges of leadership.

Some disqualifying conditions, such as dental overbite, may be corrected before entering the Academy. Candidates must not be receiving active orthodontic treatment when entering the Academy. Some of the most common medical disqualifications include: a history of asthma, exercise-induced broncho-spasm or asthmatic bronchitis, diabetes, convulsions, arrhythmias, color blindness, a history of vertigo, and hearing loss greater than 35 decibels in the speech frequencies.

Procedures to change eye refraction, including radial keratotomy (RK), photo-keratectomy (PRK), laser in situ keratomileusis (LASIK), similar surgical and non-surgical alterations to the cornea (orthokeratology), and experimental operations will disqualify the person from all Air Force Academy programs. There may be certain conditions where eye surgery may be considered for waiver.

The Academy has one of the Air Force's first PRK eye surgery facilities. Once potential pilot candidates (PPCs) are admitted, PRK is an approved surgery. Some cadets can elect for PRK eye surgery (the Air Force will pay for it), in the hope of being medically qualified vision-wise, when it comes time for selection. But no more than 10 percent of each class may get PPQ via this route. If a cadet has had this surgery, and they pass the medical evaluation one year later, they are granted a waiver to fly. (LASIK is currently not approved because the surgery leaves a flap on the eye, and the Air Force does not know how such eyes will react under G loading.) However, although a person can be disqualified from admission because of prior corrective eye surgery, a cadet, once admitted, can have such surgery, and possibly even qualify for pilot training.

Chronic skin diseases such as psoriasis, atopic dermatitis, and eczema are cause for disqualification, although waivers may be considered for some mild conditions. Any condition that could interfere with or detract from daily participation in rigorous physical training and athletic programs, wearing military equipment, or military bearing and appearance, is also disqualifying. A person who is medically disqualified may request a waiver through the Academy Admissions Office, and about half of all requests for medical waivers are granted.

REVIEW PROCESS
The Academy breaks down its applicant review process into three parts, the sum of which makes up the applicant's final score. Only those who excelled in high school

Members of a new class of cadets wait in line for in-processing at the Academy.

are likely to be selected. On average, 89 percent of first-year cadets ranked in the top 20 percent of their high school graduating class. All applicants scored high on their SATs. Twenty percent were class presidents or vice presidents, and 85 percent had earned at least one athletic letter award. Fifty-six percent were in the top 10 percent of their high school class, and 68 percent belonged to the National Honor Society.

The Academy looks for serious involvement in extracurricular activities. One cadet presented her application with straight A's. She was cadet captain of her Civil Air Patrol wing, and had various awards, including the Commander's Commendation, Honor Cadet, National Amelia Earhart Award, and the General Warren J. Barry Aerospace Education Award. In her spare time, she did volunteer work, spending more than 25 hours a school year tutoring fellow students. She volunteered with Los Niños in Mexico, and worked with the Cystic Fibrosis Foundation, and disaster relief. She was accepted into the Academy. Academic and extracurricular activities make up 60 percent of an applicant's score.

Even if an applicant does all the right things, an appointment is far from certain. One cadet earned a 3.8 grade-point average in high school. He participated in cross-country track, and worked in countless community service projects, including visiting abused and neglected kids near his home. He also participated in the Civil Air Patrol.

Still, he was not accepted to the Academy on his first try. So this young man, who had dreamed of being a pilot since kindergarten, took classes at a local college and became involved in ROTC. He applied to the Academy again, and enrolled for a year at a military prep school. He continued his community service and maintained his grades. At the prep school, he received his letter of acceptance to the Academy, where he would go on to became a soaring instructor pilot and a flight commander in the soaring program. He graduated with an appointment to flight training.

PHYSICAL APTITUDE EXAMINATION

Satisfactory completion of the physical aptitude examination (PAE) is one of the requirements for admission to the Academy, and accounts for 20 percent of the admission score. The PAE is a test of strength, agility, speed, and endurance, and is used to predict a candidate's aptitude for the Academy's physical program. The results of this test are important in the overall assessment of the

PHYSICAL APTITUDE EXAMINATION (PAE)
Pull-ups
Minimum Score = 5
Average = 10

Flexed Arm Hang (Women)
Minimum Score = 21 seconds
Average = 24 seconds

Standing Long Jump
Minimum Score Men = 6'10" (82")
Average = 7'10" (94")
Minimum Score Women = 5'8" (68")
Average = 6'02" (74")

Pushups
Minimum Score Men = 25
Average = 47
Minimum Score Women = 10
Average = 28

Kneeling Basketball Throw
Minimum Score Men = 54'
Average = 67'
Minimum Score Women = 28'
Average = 39'

300-yard shuttle run
Measures how quickly the candidate can complete six round trips between two lines spaced 25 yards apart.
Maximum Time Men = 65 seconds
Average = 60 seconds
Maximum Time Women = 75 seconds
Average = 68 seconds

candidate's admission. The examination consists of five events: pull-ups (men)/flexed-arm hang (women), standing long jump, modified basketball throw, push-ups, and a 300-yard shuttle run.

Although the PAE is pass-fail, it is imperative that all candidates perform to the best of their ability on each event. Passing with a minimum or low score either delays an offer of appointment or causes the Academy to deny an appointment, even though the individual may be otherwise fully qualified.

An interview with the admissions committee is the third part of the process. The applicant's current record is discussed, as well as their potential for success at the Academy. The committee also carefully examines each applicant's entrance essay. These factors make up the last 20 percent of the review.

Before a person may be considered for admission, they must obtain a nomination from one of their U.S. representatives or senators, the President, or the Vice President. Slots are reserved for the children of deceased or completely disabled armed forces veterans whose death or disability was service related, children of military personnel of missing-in-action or captured status, and children of Medal of Honor recipients.

There are about 4,000 cadets at the Academy at any given time. Minority students make up 17.5 percent. Women represent 14.8 percent of the entering class, a figure that mirrors the percentage of female officers in the Air Force.

BASIC CADET TRAINING (BCT)

Before cadet life begins, the commandant administers the Oath of Allegiance to the more than 1,250 cadets who enter the Academy each year. The cadet candidates then go through two 18-day periods of grueling basic cadet training (BCT), affectionately called "the Beast." This is the basic cadet's first in-your-face introduction to the structure of military life. BCT is where the cadets get a real taste of being on the lowest rung in the military pecking order. BCT is in July, before the start of the academic year.

The first part of BCT takes place in the cadet, or campus area of the Academy. This training is designed to help the applicant make the transition from a teenage civilian into military life. Since the Academy is 7,258 feet above sea level, the atmospheric pressure is lower than many cadet candidates are used to and requires extra acclimatization. Candidates are expected to report to BCT in good physical shape, and they are allowed almost no personal items—just the clothes on their back, basic

toiletries, and prescription medications cleared by the Academy physicians. The Air Force provides everything the candidates will need. If they do not report in good physical condition, the upper-class cadets will get them into shape—fast. Cadet candidates are generally not permitted to choose to withdraw, except for medical reasons, until the end of BCT.

Cadet candidates take an oath of allegiance to the United States, and are told early on to repeat to themselves, "If I can take it, I can make it. I know I can take it, therefore I can make it." They are also taught they will not make it without a buddy. Each candidate is responsible for themselves and their roommate. If one messes up, they are both penalized. Most have never been away from home, have never been in a highly stressed environment, nor have they had to think and act on their feet. The participants in BCT will learn to overcome and adapt to the challenges they will face over the next few weeks.

All the basic cadets get military haircuts: men's heads are shaved, and women's hair is cut not to go below their collars. The cadets are no longer carefree high school graduates, no longer freshmen in a civilian college. Here, they will be told there are only six basic responses 1) "Yes, sir." 2) "No, sir." 3) "Sir, I do not know." 4) "Sir, may I ask a question?" 5) "No excuse, sir." And, 6) "Sir, may I make a statement?" Until they are "recognized" later in the year, they may not use grammatical contractions (e.g., *can't, we'll, you're*) when they are talking to upper-class cadets.

A basic cadet's day begins at 0530, with upper-class cadets pounding on their doors and shouting at them to move faster. Calisthenics precede all activities, including breakfast. Basic cadets have 20 minutes to shower and clean their rooms, and for the next 36 days they are not allowed to make phone calls.

First-class cadets, or cadre, will teach the cadet candidates the basics of Air Force customs, marching, discipline, and military courtesy. Candidates take physicals and written placement tests, and learn how to shoot, clean a rifle, and drill. And, most important, they learn the Academy's honor code. All cadets take a formal course in ethics, and receive instruction in honor and ethics as part of their military training throughout the four years. Living under this code is vital to cadet development and military professionalism, but also represents an ethical maturity that will serve them all their lives.

The physical training includes strenuous exercises, running, and competitive sports, which conditions the individual to meet the physical demands of the second

"WE WILL NOT LIE, STEAL, OR CHEAT NOR TOLERATE AMONG US ANYONE WHO DOES."

The Air Force Academy honor code appears on a building at the Academy. In 1956, the first graduating class (class of 1959) formally adopted the honor code. It was then, and continues to be today, a minimum standard of conduct that cadets expect of themselves and their fellow cadets. Violators of the code are asked to resign.

part of BCT in Jack Valley, a wooded area on the Academy grounds. The basic cadet marches five miles from the "warrior ramp" located near the Vandenburg Hall dormitory to the Jack's Valley tent city.

JACK'S VALLEY

Jack's Valley, the second 18-day phase of BCT, is where the less prepared are culled out. Before candidates are formally accepted into the cadet wing in August, they must first conquer this event, affectionately called, "the Second Beast." The Second Beast is about the warrior spirit, overcoming fears, and learning to rely on one another.

Cadets about to enter their senior year are in charge of operating Jack's Valley. Organized similar to a combat

Character counts at the Academy and in the Air Force. Character is so important that there is a center for character development on the Academy grounds. The Academy defines character as: "The sum of those qualities of moral excellence, which stimulate a person to do the right thing, which is manifested through right and proper actions despite internal or external pressures to the contrary." All cadets must live by the Academy's core values: "Integrity First; Service Before Self; and Excellence in All We Do."

Cadet candidates practice hand-to-hand combat techniques with pugil sticks during basic training at Jack's Valley.

A cadet crosses a rope obstacle during basic training at Jack's Valley.

wing, they shoulder the responsibility for training, logistics support, and facilities. Permanent enlisted personnel and officers are in the background, but they stay out of the way as long as the cadets do it right.

Cadet candidates go through assault and confidence courses, and learn field skills, hand-to-hand combat techniques, and first aid. The grueling physical activities at Jack's Valley will challenge the candidates physically, mentally, and emotionally, and push them to their physical limits. One daunting challenge is a 20-obstacle confidence course designed to test physical and mental strength. Candidates go in looking worried, and come out looking confident—this is where the Academy begins to build confidence and teamwork in its future officers and pilots. Much of the strength candidates need comes

from within, and the rest emerges as the individuals become a team.

Teamwork is one of the most important lessons of BCT. While some individuals will not be able to overcome certain of the challenges, all will be pressed to standards beyond their perceived limitations, pushed to the breaking point. They will quickly discover that success comes only from teamwork.

Groups of 10 basic cadets are presented a problem, and they must find a solution. Each group is given two boards, a rope, and six sandbag "bombs." The task: go over a fence topped with barbed wire, and pass the six bombs to the other side—without touching the fence. During one recent exercise, every group that charged into the exercise without taking time to plan failed. Those that

23

spent too much time planning ran out of their allotted 15 minutes. However, one group made it. While being forced by cadre to sing, "You Are My Sunshine," the group tied the boards together, formed a human pyramid, and accomplished the mission—with 30 seconds to spare.

The last part of the training is a march to the main Academy area, where the surviving basic cadets receive shoulder boards signifying their official acceptance into the cadet wing. Most basic cadets find the motivation to make it through BCT, although 50 to 70 in each class will withdraw. The survivors become "doolies."

FOURTH-CLASS CADET

In Air Force terms, *Doolie* is slang for "fourth-class cadet." It is a pejorative term, and stands for someone insignificant, whose rank is measured in negative units, and who will graduate in some time approaching infinity.

The doolie's first day at the Academy is the day after acceptance, a Thursday. The day is packed with activity. Cadets will pick up uniforms, sign out computers, receive roommate assignments, and clean their dormitory rooms. There are two dormitories, Vandenburg Hall and Sijan Hall. The facilities are co-ed, where cadets sleep two to a room, although males and females are separated. Cadets are organized into roughly 120-person "squadrons" in the dormitories. Doolies are subjected to one year of constant mental training administered by upper-class cadets and are continuously memorizing disjointed facts. They can be stopped anywhere, any time, and have questions barked at them, just inches from their nose, while they are "braced" at rigid attention. Questions may range from military history and current events to the menu for the next four meals. Correct answers do not get rewards; incorrect answers get extra drilling and calisthenics.

Everything is regimented and timed for doolies, even leisure activities. Students wear uniforms to class, military dress during training, and dress uniforms to all formal events. From sunrise to sunset, the cadets march, attend classes, have study periods, and take exams. Even eating is regimented. There is one hour for assembly and meals. All cadets eat together in Mitchell Hall and, in reality, get about 25 minutes of the hour to eat. Doolies get even less time, since they eat braced, and are continually asked questions from upper-class cadets throughout the meal. Eating a meal is a challenge for doolies, who must keep their eyes straight ahead, and at some tables may be required to chew each mouthful exactly seven times before swallowing. They are admonished for more than seven chews, and may have chews subtracted from the next mouthful. But there is always a point to this, and to all training. Over time, the cadet learns to pay attention to details. In addition, doolies rotate between dining tables, so the "training" is spread around.

"The worst experience I had in my doolie year," said one Air Force F-15E Strike Eagle pilot, "was dealing with the stress. About mid-year, I had four papers due, two

Above: Cadet squadrons compete against each other in a race on Field Day at the Academy.

Right: Brigadier General John Weida, the Academy commandant, joins cadets on the first leg of the 35-mile relay Warrior Run, which was added to basic cadet training in 2003. "The Warrior Run is the ultimate event in reinforcing the benefits of team over self," said Weida. "None of the basic cadets could complete the run on their own. But together, running relay over approximately 35 miles of rugged terrain, they can accomplish their goal."

25

Cadets solve algebra problems during study hour in their dormitory. Each cadet has a roommate and mandatory daily study hours called "academic call to quarters" from 1900 to 2230 hours.

or three tests, and two or three projects, plus my military training. In addition, I had to be washed, dressed, room made up, and finished with breakfast by 6:30 every morning."

The regimentation, stress, and overload quickly cull out the less prepared. The class of 2003 had 1,335 entering doolies. That number was down to 1,173 at the beginning of the second year. By graduation, only 974 had survived. Cadets must, with very few exceptions, graduate in four years. Since 1990, attrition has averaged about 20 percent for each graduating class.

Once accepted, the cadet receives a free four-year education and about $600 a month in pay. But there is really nothing free in life. The cadet pays their expenses— uniforms, laundry, football tickets, haircuts, and so forth. Doolies will receive about $80 after expenses. But this improves over the cadet's four years. Third-class cadets receive about $220 after expenses. Second-class cadets receive about $340, and first-class cadets receive almost $600 a month. However, the cadets will all pay in varying degrees over the four years in emotional stress, physical exhaustion, and academic overload, even during parts of their summer vacations.

RECOGNITION

In mid-March, doolies will undergo the worst 48 hours of their stay at the Academy. They spend a weekend in physically exhausting exercise—a flashback to BCT. After their bodies are no longer willing to function, they can only draw strength from their minds to keep themselves going. Throughout the 48 grueling hours, the point is to reinforce the individual's behavior of acting composed, cool, and rational when placed in stressful situations.

The last event of the 48 hours is the "run to the rock." All the senior cadets join the doolies on a 3 1/2-mile run to Cathedral Rock. Once there, the doolies' year of trial is over. When they return to their rooms, they discover that the upper-class cadets have cleaned their rooms and pressed all their uniforms. That evening, each squadron holds a ceremony in which the fourth-class cadets are "pinned" with their prop and wings insignia. Later they will have their first meal at rest. The fourth-class cadets have spent a year learning to follow; now they must learn to lead.

ACADEMY AIRMANSHIP PROGRAMS

All cadets participate in some form of air activity in each of their four years, and the airmanship programs are a vital part of a future pilot's course of study. The 557th Flying Training Squadron conducts all airmanship training at the academy. Twenty-one courses cover basic and advanced instruction in gliders, parachuting, and single-engine airplane flight. A soaring curriculum is run by senior cadets, with a flying club and a flying team that competes against 144 colleges nationwide.

This cadet must learn to crawl through mud before he learns to fly.

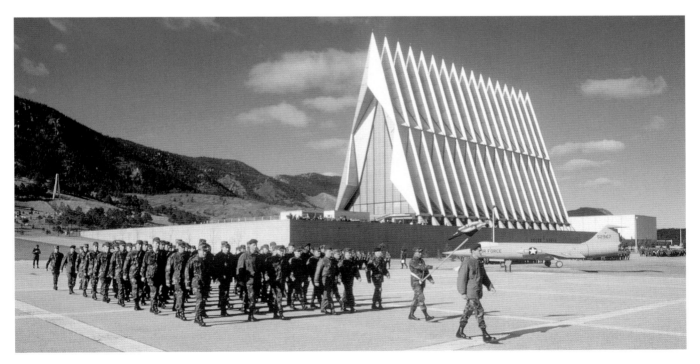

A cadet squadron marches in front of the Air Force Academy chapel.

Sports audiences across the country are delighted by the aerobatics of the falcon, the flying mascot of the U.S. Air Force Academy. Twelve cadets typically participate in this extracurricular activity, with four new falconer trainees chosen from each new class to replace graduating seniors. The new falconers begin training in January under the leadership of experienced upperclassmen and the officer-in-charge.

This first-class cadet lets Liberty catch a food-laden lure during falcon training. The Academy mascots dive for their dinner at speeds exceeding 200 miles per hour. The Academy has 10 to 12 falcon mascots.

A cadet making a parachute jump. After completing five such jumps and the basic parachuting course, cadets are eligible for advanced training and a chance to join the Wings of Blue parachute team. Four parachute programs are offered in the cadet airmanship program: basic, advanced, instructor/jumpmaster training, and instructor/jumpmaster duty. In these courses, more than 20,000 jumps are made each year. The basic course trains over 750 cadets annually. The final course gives military training credit to cadets who are instructors for the other three programs. Cadets play a major role in training and safety. For example, cadet jumpmasters control virtually all cadet jumps. These duties provide practical leadership experience with significant responsibility.

All third-class cadets receive instruction in flying a two-seat sailplane to enable them to solo in conventional and powered sailplane flights. Air Force pilots supervise the soaring program, but cadets run it. After the sophomore year, cadets will spend part of a summer at an operational Air Force base. There they will get a firsthand look at how the Air Force functions. Some may even get a variety of orientation flights. Second-class cadets (juniors) participate in parachuting and navigation. Advanced courses in these areas prepare students to be instructors, and permit them to gain operational and leadership experience.

Flying activities are complemented by academic studies in astronomy, aeronautics, astronautics, and physics. Also, any cadet may belong to the Cadet Aviation Club, and fly light aircraft as a member of the club.

CADET PILOT TRAINING

The Academy started training pilots in the 1960s, but the program was suspended in 1997 after three cadets and

Two second-class cadets compare notes before a glider flight.

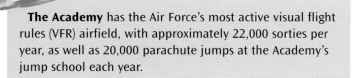

The Academy has the Air Force's most active visual flight rules (VFR) airfield, with approximately 22,000 sorties per year, as well as 20,000 parachute jumps at the Academy's jump school each year.

three officer instructor pilots (IPs) died in accidents. Subsequently, the Air Force started to see attrition rates skyrocket at JSUPT bases. In 1998, the Air Force started sending cadets and recent graduates to fixed base operators (FBOs) around the country for introductory flight training (IFT). This improved the attrition rates, but the Air Force realized that without direct military oversight, a critical part of training future military pilots was missing.

Attrition rates were not the only concern for the Air Force. The goal of IFT is to screen for success at JSUPT. IFT primarily screens for three problems: attitude, aptitude, and airsickness. The most important is attitude. The Air Force works with students to overcome the other two if possible. "Attitude problems are not tolerated," said Lieutenant Colonel Phillip Beaudoin, commander of the 557th Flying Training Squadron at the Academy. "Go to IFT with the desire to succeed and to work (as with any other flight training program)."

This cadet wears glider pilot wings and appears to be enjoying himself high above the Academy.

The upper-class cadet on the left has her parachute and glider-instructor wings and gives a newer cadet some pointers.

A group of cadets in the parachuting program look toward the sky to wait for skydivers to appear. The Air Force Academy's 94th Airmanship Training Squadron molds leaders through soaring and parachuting programs.

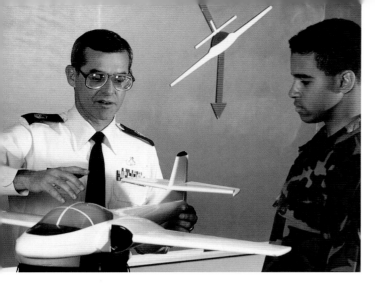

A senior master sergeant instructor, left, holds a model of a T-37 Tweet aircraft as he reviews basic flight concepts with a cadet. The sergeant is a member of the 50th Airmanship Training Squadron.

USAFA TG-3 landing with an AF Thunderbird paint scheme. The TG-3A (Schweizer 1-26) is a single-seat, medium-performance sailplane used for cross-country and spin training. The TG-3A allowed students to master basic flight maneuvers and solo before progressing to more advanced gliders. It was recently replaced by the TG-10C Sailplane (Blanik L-13AC). Note the spoiler on the left wing, used to cancel the lift on the wings for landings.

A glider being towed to altitude. It generally takes about 12 rides in this glider for a student to be ready to solo.

The Air Force felt that including some aspects of military pilot training in the USAFA's curriculum, such as formal stand-up briefs, pilot checklists, and standards for reacting to emergencies, would better prepare cadets for JSUPT. Plus, an "on-base" program would provide more time for their busy schedules.

Currently, the U.S. Air Force Academy's IFT is conducted on the Academy grounds as well as off-site at private airfields within immediate commuting distance of the Academy. The plan is eventually to return all IFT to the Academy. The Academy currently does not have the capacity to train all 500-plus pilot candidates to a PPC level. However, when the new program takes effect, the Academy will be able to accommodate all cadets.

All of the off-site IPs are civilian-certified flight instructors (CFIs). At the USAFA, most IPs are civilian CFIs who fly under the supervision of a military cadre. A few military CFIs fly for quality assurance. Diamond Aircraft Industries of Ontario, Canada, and Embry Riddle Aeronautical University teamed up to win a contract to provide pilot training for Academy cadets. Diamond is providing 35 DA20-C1 Falcons, modified with the stick on the right. The configuration allows students to use the throttle with the left hand, as they will do in JSUPT. Other FBOs use any aircraft allowed by FAR Part 61 or 141. Typically, Cessnas or Pipers fit the bill.

Cadets who are selected for JSUPT may complete IFT before graduation, if slots are available. If not, they do so after graduation, as slots become available.

SOAR-FOR-ALL PROGRAM

The Academy's Soar-for-All year-round soaring program is the largest and most active glider operation in the world. It is designed to teach cadets the basic concepts of flying, and encourage them to become pilots. All cadets attend ground school instruction taught by second-class cadets. Each cadet attends approximately 30 hours of training where they learn basic aerodynamics, weather, takeoff and landing patterns, and radio work.

The cadets' first soaring experience is in the TG-14 motorglider, which familiarizes them with aircraft controls, the ever-present checklist, and pattern work. This is followed by unpowered flight in a TG-10D, the aircraft in which most cadets will solo, or the TG-10B Super Blanik L-23 glider. Over 25,000 sorties are flown in this program annually, and nearly 1,000 solos are made each year. The average student takes about 12 sorties to solo. There are 12 Blanik TG-10Bs, 5 TG-10Cs (L-13s), and 4 TG-10Ds

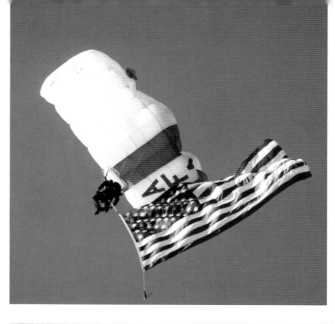

A member of the Wings of Blue cadet parachute team delivers the flag at an Academy sporting event.

33

(L-33s) gliders, and 14 TG-14 Super Ximango motorgliders available to the cadets for initial and intermediate soaring cross-country training.

"Since the gliders are unpowered," said one cadet, "the only way to go fast is to drop the nose. That puts you closer to the ground, and that is not good. The toughest thing isn't flying or landing, but taking off. There is nothing harder or more gut wrenching than trying to fly formation while attached to an airplane with 200 feet of cable between you and it, in bumpy conditions. Of course, after altitude is reached, you release from tow and the rest is easy. In the end, I had 11 flights, two airsickness incidents, and one pair of solo wings."

CADET INSTRUCTORS

Outstanding second-year cadets may compete for qualification as cadet instructors in the Soar-for-All glider program. Applicants are selected to go through upgrade training to begin in the fall and continuing through spring. They are required to be medically qualified, and are selected based on an interview and flying skills demonstrated during the Soar-for-All program. They must also pass the instructor upgrade course consisting of 40 hours of academic coursework and 80 to 100 training flights. They will spend considerable time at the airfield and must have a minimum GPA and MPA of 2.6. During their second-class year (junior year) they serve one summer period and the academic year as an instructor while performing non-commissioned-officer-type duties in the squadron. As first-class cadets (senior year), they serve one summer period and the academic year as instructors while holding soaring leadership positions.

Ground school lessons follow a sequential path toward becoming a cadet instructor, starting with the basics of the airplane and finishing with checkride preparation at the end of the semester. The course is offered in the third class year, and the final project is a qualification checkride.

The cadet instructor force consists of about 160 sailplane instructor pilots. Essential to the Soar-for-All program is the cadet instructor pilot upgrade course. Eighty third-class cadets are selected from about 400 applicants for this semester-long program. The selection is based upon their flying ability and on academic and military performance. These upgrade instructors must accumulate at least 100 Soar-for-All instructional sorties, plus many hours of strenuous ground school before they qualify to wear instructor pilot wings. Upgrade instructors volunteer their time after school and on weekends.

These sacrifices demand a lot of time and dedication from the cadet instructors, since most of them are taking over 23 credit hours of academics.

The Academy keeps the cadet instructor pilots motivated and proficient by offering them glider aerobatics, with ground and flight instruction to include spins, aerobatic maneuvers, precision flying techniques, and competition rules towards attaining USAFA cadet spin IP and demonstration pilot ratings. Qualified cadets may be selected to travel to aerobatic competitions and air shows, and participate in home football game aerial demonstrations, as part of the Academy's soaring demonstration team.

In the cross-country soaring program, ground school includes instructions in regulations, planning, weather, thermalling techniques, competition rules, and equipment use. Flight training includes precision and off-field landings, thermalling techniques, dual and solo cross-country, and competition sorties. Qualified cadets may be selected to compete in cross-country soaring competitions.

USAFA FLYING TEAM

The USAFA Flying Team competes in intercollegiate flying competition events at regional and two National Intercollegiate Flying Association Safety and Flight Evaluation conferences each year. In addition, the USAFA Flying Team offers cadets realistic Air Force flying and operational experience.

About 40 to 50 cadets apply for the USAFA Flying Team each year, and candidates must complete a demanding membership selection process. The screening process begins with fourth-class cadets, who must have a PPC, not be on academic probation, and must have a minimum GPA of 2.5 to be considered. With these initial requirements met, the remaining cadets are given computer accuracy, simulated comprehensive aircraft navigation, aircraft identification, preflight, and navigation tests to measure their knowledge base of these areas. Cadets take a series of two tests; and both their overall score and their improvement from one battery of tests to the next are considered. Following the initial cut, about 15 to 18 cadets are interviewed, during which the entire team drills applicants with questions to narrow the field even more. After the interviews, approximately 12 cadets remain.

During the spring semester, the fourth-class cadet team member prospects are enrolled in a class in which they study precision landings, cross-country navigation,

The T-41 aircraft are used by the Academy's flying club.

A staff sergeant instructor points out a feature of the T-37 mockup to a cadet.

Graduation day sends hats flying in the air and brings new responsibilities to the newly minted second lieutenants. The Thunderbirds roar overhead during the event.

aircraft preflight, instrument flying, message drop, aircraft identification, Federal Aviation Administration (FAA) regulations, the *Aeronautical Information Manual*, and USAF flying regulations. After several class sessions, cadets take written tests to measure their performance in the upgrade process. At this point, they also take a screening flight with an IP in either a T-41D (Cessna 172) or a Cessna 150 to get a general feel for the prospective member's piloting skills and to ensure they will not be unsafe in the aircraft. The USAFA Flying Team's resources include three T-41D and three C-150 aircraft. Each year they fly over 55,000 sorties.

Just before the spring break training camp, the final cut is made, and five or six fourth-class cadets are selected to become full-fledged flying team members. The new flying team cadets are trained to fly the team's aircraft during their third summer-training period. Training consists of intense ground school lessons and eight training flights with an Air Force officer IP. Each cadet takes a checkride with an Air Force flight evaluator at the completion of the summer training program. This checkride is the culmination of nearly one year of hard work. After successfully completing the checkride, new team members begin practicing flying competition events on a regular basis, honing their skills to become national champions.

FLIGHT RATINGS

First-class cadets who are medically qualified for pilot training and are selected to enter JSUPT after graduation, must take the IFT course, in which they receive dual and solo flight training to complete the requirements for an FAA PPC. This course is only open to cadets who do not already possess a PPC and have not declined pilot training. Cadets who decline pilot training after starting IFT are removed from the course. Cadets who drop IFT after starting, or cannot meet requirements, lose eligibility for JSUPT. This training includes a maximum of 50 hours of flight training and FAA-approved ground school, which results in a PPC. This prescreening helps Academy officials decide if a cadet has the "right stuff" to make it through JSUPT.

The Air Force Thunderbirds salute the new graduates with an aerial demonstration.

COMBAT SURVIVAL TRAINING (CST)

Every summer, third class cadets spend two three-week periods of the nine weeks of their summer at the Academy. The summer is broken down into three programs: combat survival training, global engagement, and either soaring, jump school, or flying team upgrade. Global engagement is a nine-day-long course that introduces cadets to the Expeditionary Air Force concept of deploying to a crisis situation, establishing a bare-base operation, executing the mission, and re-deploying home. CST and global engagement are required for graduation and must be taken by all cadets.

At the end of their first year, the former doolies go directly to CST. This three-week course shows cadets—and future pilots—what they must do to survive in various terrains and outdoor situations.

CST consists of four days of survival training, followed by three days of evasion training, conducted in Saylor Park, an off-campus facility. The training scenario is that the cadet is a downed pilot behind enemy lines, trying to evade capture. Upper-class cadre teach the cadets (about 10 to a group) techniques that range from clothing and environments to what a downed pilot may and may not eat or drink. It is a huge geography lesson, mixed with survival common sense.

During these seven days, each day consists of one meal. The first day, the meal may be three rabbits split among 10 people. "The rabbits are very small and don't have much meat," said one cadet. "In addition, lots of vegetables came with the rabbits. The vegetables were our only source of food for the next day also."

A cadet is hoisted from the water during combat survival training (CST) at the Academy.

A cadet participates in CST at the Academy.

An instructor demonstrates animal skinning techniques during CST for cadets.

administer basic first aid, and basic evasion techniques. "For food that day, we had rice with some ground beef hash," said one cadet.

The fourth day consists of a 4-kilometer hike (about 2.5 miles), again without a trail. The cadets learn triangulation using compasses and maps.

The next day is spent navigating and learning evasion techniques, such as using camouflage, movement, hand signs, and more ground navigation. That evening the cadets will hike another four kilometers in the pitch dark.

The last three days and nights are devoted to evasion tactics. Cadets are divided into three-person groups, given a detailed map of the area and a target destination, and must elude the "aggressors" (upper-class cadre), and reach the target destination by 0700 hours.

During the first two days, the cadets learn some basic signaling skills, as well as how to construct shelters, build a fire, tie knots, and purify water from a mud hole using iodine tablets.

The second night is spent on a night navigation (night nav) exercise. The night nav is a two-kilometer hike, usually in the pitch dark, with no trail, over mountainous terrain.

The third day, cadets learn how to set small-game traps, and how to distinguish which plants are edible and which ones are not. They cross obstacles (fences, roads, train tracks), learn how to use the global positioning system (GPS), how to

Cadets wade into the water during CST at the Academy.

A cadet hoists his sword during a ceremony at the Academy.

A B-2 bomber flies over the chapel at the Air Force Academy.

Students can also earn advanced ratings, such as a commercial pilot rating through the airmanship program, with a PPC being a prerequisite. Dual-flight instruction is also available to complete the requirements for an FAA instrument pilot rating. Again, a PPC is a prerequisite. An airplane flight instructor rating is also available, although an FAA commercial pilot certificate is a prerequisite. This training is conducted at the Academy's Aero Club at the cadet's expense, although some subsidy is available from the Cadet Aviation Club.

GRADUATION

The happiest day of a cadet's life is graduation day— the beginning of an exciting military career. Each cadet graduates with a bachelor of science degree, a commission as a second lieutenant in the United States Air Force, and a secret security clearance. Officers agree to serve for at least eight years after graduation, five of which must be on active duty. They agree to serve for 10 years if they become pilots. Officers who fail to complete any period of active duty may incur a liability to reimburse the U.S. Government for an appropriate proportion of the cost of their Academy education, which is currently about $36,000 per year. For those selected for flight training, the next step is JSUPT.

In 1976, the Academy admitted the first class that included women. That class graduated in 1980. From it came the first woman to pilot Air Force Two, the vice president's airplane, and the first military woman to inhabit the International Space Station.

TWO

Pilot Training

Joint Specialized Undergraduate Pilot Training (JSUPT) is the Air Force's flight training program that qualifies Air Force, Navy, and Marine officers, as military aviators. The Air Education Training Command (AETC) provides this training at four Air Force bases, the largest of which is the 47th Flying Training Wing at Laughlin Air Force Base, Texas. The other units providing training are the 14th Flying Training Wing at Columbus Air Force Base, Mississippi; the 71st Flying Training Wing at Vance Air Force Base, Oklahoma; and the 479th Flying Training Group at Moody Air Force Base, Georgia.

Becoming an Air Force pilot is an honor that must be earned, and there are no guarantees in flight school. Recently, of 30 students who started JSUPT at Laughlin Air Force Base, 22 earned their silver wings.

Phase I, which lasts six weeks, is mostly academics. Twelve-hour days are the norm. Phase II is conducted on the flightline, and Phase III is "track select," where students are selected for advanced training in specified aircraft. JSUPT students accomplish primary training in the T-37 Tweet or the T-6A "Texan II." About half the students fly the T-6 Texan II, which is transitioning into the training fleet as the Tweet's eventual replacement.

A 44th Fighter Squadron pilot scans the sky for adversary aircraft from the cockpit of an F-15 Eagle during a training exercise.

STUDENT PROFILE

Most students are in their mid-20s and have 70 to 250 flying hours in their civilian logbooks. Students must arrive at JSUPT before their 30th birthday. Each student's PPC indicates that they know how to fly a small civilian airplane and that they have a sense of situational awareness (SA), an important part of flying. Students also do things the civilian way. Military flying is vastly different from civilian flying. Students must learn new radio procedures, traffic patterns, emergency responses, formation flying, and more. The Air Force teaches these students how to fly "the Air Force way," and things will move fast. One hundred sixty knots is equivalent to about 30 seconds on a final approach, a lot faster than the approximately 60-knot approach speed of a Cessna 150, the airplane that students probably learned to fly as a civilian. The basic airspeed in the T-38 Talon jet trainer is 300 knots, and it routinely flies at 400 knots. Students have to be 100-percent involved in what the aircraft is doing, every second. And students must stay ahead of the airplane, anticipating where it is heading, and correcting if it is not going where planned.

Graduates of the Air Force Academy and Air Force ROTC/OTS comprise most of the approximately 15 classes of about 30 students each that matriculate each year at JSUPT. Many pilots who come from OTS are training for the Air Force Reserve or Air National Guard pilot assignments, and they receive exactly the same training as active Air Force pilots.

A five-hour "top-off" program is required for JSUPT students if more than two years have elapsed between their last checkride or flight review and their JSUPT start date. During these five hours, students must receive a flight review in accordance with Federal Aviation Regulation Part 61.56, in which their flying habits and maneuvers are evaluated.

A student's aircraft egress method is observed in a simulator and graded by an evaluator.

On April 6, 1917, the day Congress declared war on Germany, the United States had fewer than 250 airplanes, all of which were obsolete, and 56 pilots. By November 11, 1918, Armistice Day, 8,689 cadets had graduated from primary flight schools. In addition, schools in Europe had trained 1,674 men as pilots and 851 as observers. Flight training had its price, however. On average, one man was killed in an airplane accident for every 18 fully trained flying officers.

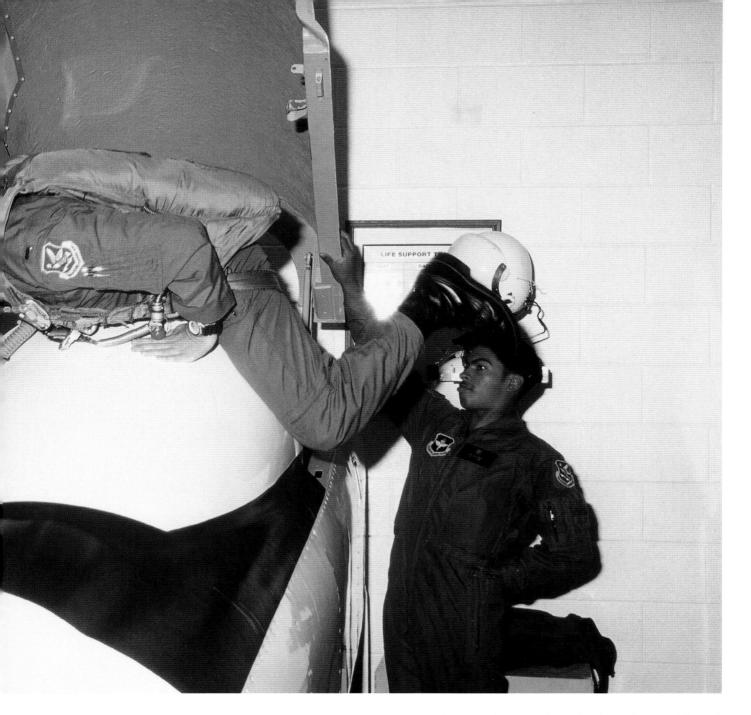

JSUPT—PHASE I

Upon arrival at a JSUPT base, students spend about two-and-a-half days in introductory briefings. This relatively short and boring period is called "death by briefing." Before students actually get any "stick-time," they must attend six weeks of ground school and academics, called "slackademics" because of its routine and laid-back nature, compared to what's ahead for the student on the flightline. During this period, students learn aerodynamics, engine systems, basic weather, navigation, overhead traffic patterns and rules, safety, emergency procedures, and more. They also learn how to file and close military flight plans, which are different from civilian flight plans.

Military flight plans are filed on a DD Form-175 and submitted to the resident base operations, or base ops, for input into the air traffic control (ATC) system. Generally, military pilots do not interact with civilian flight service stations (FSS) unless they are stopping over at an airfield with no base ops—that is, a non-military airfield.

Students' days are filled with aerospace physiology classes, practicing parachute landing falls, and parasailing.

This is serious training. In aerospace physiology, students experience the altitude chamber, learn how to ground egress from the jet, and practice ejection procedures. Students need a stack of books over a foot high—all for just the first six months. Despite the straightforward nature of the academics in Phase I, the 12-hour days and sheer volume of tasks to be accomplished can be overwhelming.

The less prepared are quickly culled from the ranks. Students who score less than 85 percent on three of the eight academic tests are subject to a commander's review board. This elimination process sends some students packing early.

THE ALTITUDE CHAMBER

Most Air Force aircraft are pressurized, but a pilot must recognize when he is about to experience oxygen starvation, commonly called hypoxia. Several factors determine how much oxygen a person needs, and when they start losing consciousness from lack of oxygen. This varies with each individual, depending on height, body weight, and other factors.

At a simulated 35,000 feet, students practice "pressure breathing." At that altitude, the partial pressure of oxygen is too low to be absorbed into the blood. The altitude chamber's oxygen system forces oxygen into a student's mouth at a higher pressure, to diffuse it into the

Planning a flight will always be one of the most important things a pilot will do.

Students will learn how to use night-vision goggles (NVG). While not creating daylight, the goggles amplify existing light, and everything appears with a greenish tint.

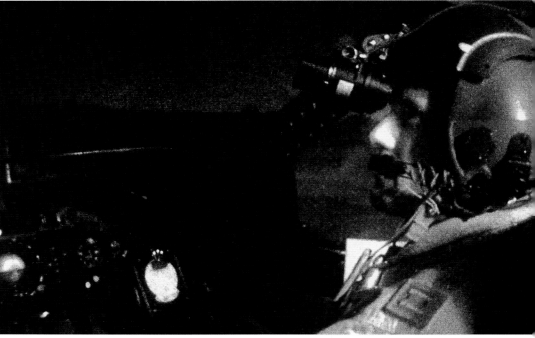

The T-6A Texan II will eventually replace the aging T-37 Tweet.

blood. Breathing is no longer automatic. Students have to think about breathing, forcefully exhaling, and passively inhaling.

At a simulated 25,000 feet, students will remove their masks and begin to experience hypoxia. The first symptoms are unique to each individual, but usually include a tingly feeling, followed by disorientation.

At a simulated 18,000 feet, the instructor tells the students to again remove their masks for a night-vision demonstration. Students are told to study maps, although they will not have an accurate visual read on the detail and color due to the effects of oxygen depletion. When they replace their masks and resume breathing oxygen, all the detail and color that was not visible to them when they were not breathing supplemental oxygen now appears on the map. This demonstrates the importance of ensuring good oxygen flow during night operations.

The last test in the chamber is a rapid decompression. Students sit at sea level atmosphere, and then *boom!*, they are suddenly at 10,000 feet. Their ears clog, and the air is instantly misty because the air vapor condensed. For every 1,000 feet of altitude there is a 2-degree Celsius drop in temperature, which will condense the air vapor.

SPATIAL DISORIENTATION

A pilot suffering spatial disorientation is likely to end up dead unless they have been trained to recognize the onset of symptoms. Without a visible horizon (while flying in clouds at night, for example, or turning in a dogfight) the senses cannot be trusted; the inner ears take over and upset the pilot's equilibrium. To demonstrate, the instructor spins a student in the Barany (or spin) chair, which has a seat belt. The student shuts their eyes, and bows their head. After about 20 seconds, the inner ear stabilizes, and the student no longer feels the spinning. When the chair stops spinning, the instructor tells the

The tandem seats in the Texan II do not allow the IP to reach all of the student's instruments.

An external view of an altitude chamber, from where students are monitored.

The altitude chamber is a sealed room in which pressure can be changed to simulate any altitude, from sea level to extreme high altitude. There are oxygen mask hookups for each student.

student to open their eyes and sit up, with arms above them. The student feels like they are tumbling forward, and without the seatbelt, they would fall out of the chair. Spatial disorientation in a low-flying aircraft could prove fatal. The pilot's natural inclination is to make rapid stick inputs, which could lead to a stall, or much worse, a spin, which could cause the pilot to lose control and crash.

SYSTEMS

About 10 days into JSUPT, students start studying aircraft systems. If something goes wrong in the air, knowing the aircraft's systems helps the pilot isolate and correct the problem. They study aircraft limitations, flight instruments, communication and navigation systems, engine mechanics, canopy and ejection systems, and more. The questions students must be able to answer before ever sitting in the cockpit range from the simple, "What is the nominal takeoff gross weight of the T-37?" (7,000 pounds), to the more complex, "What three components use the 115-volt AC 3 phase bus?" (heading indicator, attitude indicator, and radio navigation). Students must complete 30 hours of computer-aided instruction, and receive constant reviews from the instructors. The first

academic course, T-37 Systems, has a 30-question test. The study material is the first 50 pages of the technical order for the T-37B Tweet. The consequence of poor time management can mean elimination from JSUPT early.

Throughout this period, students should be conditioning their bodies for the stresses of the excess Gs created by high-speed flight maneuvers. The fighter aircrew conditioning test (FACT) measures students' ability to take excessive Gs. It consists of 10 to 15 slow repetitions of arm curls, bench presses, lat pull downs, leg presses, and leg curls. Then, with one minute for each exercise, students do 20 to 50 pushups, 30 to 50 sit-ups, and 20 to 50 free squats. All the weights for the strength exercises are based on a percentage of a student's body weight.

SIMULATORS

Long before actual flying takes place, students experience things that can go wrong in a flight, but in the safety of a controlled situation, in simulators. A simulator can throw many problems at the students to test their levels of knowledge, and give them important practice in how to react to malfunctioning systems and in-flight emergencies.

The 12th Operations Support Squadron (OSS) oversees pilot and navigator simulator training. Contract civilians are employed as computer maintenance technicians. Console operators help set up realistic scenarios used in the program.

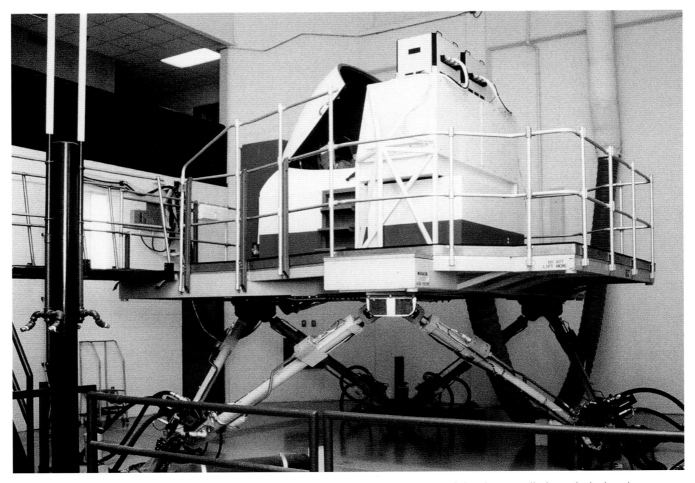

Exterior view of the T-37 flight simulator. Ground and air egress training is an integral part of the Air Force pilot's survival education.

About a week before students take their "dollar ride" (their first ride with an instructor), they take several simulator rides. Although students have a PPC and can fly, the Tweet or the Texan II is not the Cessna or Piper that students learned to fly. The Tweet and Texan II are much faster, and are easy to over-control. Simulators are used first to give students a feel for the airplane in a safe environment. By the time students strap into an actual Tweet or Texan II, they will have "taken off" and "landed" several times in two three-hour simulator sessions, during which they have gained a good idea of their strengths and weaknesses.

Simulators are used to test students' skills, and to challenge them with new situations. Usually, the next simulator ride does not go as well as the previous ride. The instructor may tell students to hop in and start flying, without getting to do the checklists or start the engines. It is designed to throw the students' rhythm off, and students continue to make new mistakes with each simulation. The primary teaching point is to get the student to adapt to different situations.

Students have been learning the general subjects, including ground operations, takeoff, departure, climb, level-off, clearing turns, radio procedures, trim, throttle techniques, situational awareness, in-flight planning, and VOR operation. VOR (very high frequency omni-range) is a basic electronic navigation technique that relies on ground-based transmitters that emit signals to a VOR receiver on board the aircraft. The reception of VHF signals is in a line of sight, and the aircraft receiver must be at a minimum altitude of 1,000 feet above ground level (AGL) in order to pick up a VOR signal.

There is a constant flow of traffic between classrooms, mockups, and simulators. Classroom time involves

Using T-37 models, an IP debriefs a student pilot after a training sortie.

A view inside the cockpit of a T-37 Tweet aircraft as an instructor pilot (IP) performs a roll maneuver during pilot training at Vance Air Force Base.

An aerial close-up view of a T-37 Tweet aircraft from the 71st Flying Training Wing, 8th Flying Training Squadron "Eightballers," Vance Air Force Base, Oklahoma.

studying the gradebook, which contains records of pilot syllabus lessons, academic tests, briefings, flights and checkrides, and other information on students. The gradebook shell is pre-assembled and given to students as they begin a phase of flying training. Students are responsible for keeping their gradebooks current and well organized as they complete events and receive gradesheets or other documentation of their training progress. The gradebook reinforces the point that everything must be documented. Even if students fly exactly as the Air Force wants them to, if the gradebook does not make the grade, they do not make the grade.

JSUPT—PHASE II

At this point, there is about a 12 percent washout rate. Those who did not study hard in Phase I are gone. It is now show time, and surviving students look forward to the day they take their first flight. The 12-hour days on the flightline are a solid 12 hours. Students bring their lunch to the flightline, or they go without a meal until the

An IP with the 71st Flying Training Wing sits in the cockpit of a T-37 Tweet aircraft with a student, at Vance Air Force Base.

evening. It is the culmination of weeks of intensive study, hard work, simulator rides, and exams. Now, however, the pressure only becomes more intense. Students begin the day as early as 0500 hours, spending their time learning the routines crucial to becoming an Air Force pilot: flying, studying, taking exams, and checkrides. At Sheppard Air Force Base, for example, each student gets about 120 hours of flight time, and 20 hours of simulator time as they begin to learn how to fly a T-37 Tweet or a T-6A Texan II.

T-37B "TWEET"

The T-37B Tweet is an unpressurized, twin-engine jet with side-by-side seating. It is used in teaching students the fundamentals of aircraft handling, instrument navigation, and formation flying. In the Tweet, students learn to execute stalls, basic aerobatics, overhead traffic patterns and landings, pattern entry, straight-in patterns, pattern breakout, simulated engine failures from both high and low altitude, and missed approaches. Students' 12-hour days are filled with flying and high-stress emergency procedures training. The intensity of the training is beyond that of college, because students must retain every scrap of information they learn here for the rest of their career. They refer to it as "drinking from a firehose," because there is so much to learn and assimilate in a short time.

T-6A TEXAN II

The T-6A Texan II is the Air Force's newest trainer, a pressurized, two-seat (tandem) single-engine turboprop aircraft. A turboprop is a propeller aircraft driven by a jet turbine engine. The Texan II also incorporates the newest avionics with a "glass" cockpit, which feature instrument displays in a very different design from the Tweet's round dials and gauges.

The first phase of T-6A training is similar to that in the Tweet; it is ground based, where students learn about human physiological limitations as they pertain to flight. During this phase, students learn the importance of their emergency equipment and proper operation of the T-6's ejection seat.

There are some differences between the Texan II and the Tweet. The big difference is that in the T-6A, the instructor sits behind the student, and the student controls many of the instruments the instructor cannot reach. To compensate for this, T-6 students are given more simulator time than their counterparts' training on the T-37. Both the T-37 and the T-6A have dual controls, and an exact duplicate set of instruments.

The Texan II has a Martin Baker Mk. 16 ejection seat with zero-zero capability, which is a significant improvement over the seats in the T-37. Zero-zero is almost the lowest point in the ejection envelope, sitting on the ground, with the aircraft immobile—not recommended. A zero-zero ejection seat launches a normal sized pilot to a height of over 200 feet, and gives him a full chute in around three seconds.

The Tweet ejection seat has a two-stage trigger mechanism, which requires the pilot to raise the ejection grips to uncover the triggers before squeezing them. It is ballistically propelled rather than rocket-powered as in most other jet aircraft. The recommended minimum ejection altitude for all Air Force aircraft under controlled flight is 2,000 feet AGL. If the aircraft is in uncontrolled flight—that is, a spin—the recommended minimum ejection altitude is 10,000 feet AGL. This means that if an aircraft becomes uncontrolled below 10,000 feet AGL, the pilot should eject immediately.

Ejection procedures vary slightly with each aircraft. For example, in the F-15E, ejection on takeoff would only be above 50 knots indicated air speed (KIAS). In T-38s, it is 75 KIAS, since the T-38 seat has a zero altitude and a 50 knot envelope. If the aircraft is airborne, the students are taught to try to get to 250 KIAS and 500 feet AGL using whatever energy the aircraft has left before ejecting. Naturally, if the student or pilot can abort or recover the

IPs compare logbooks after a training mission. A T-37 Tweet aircraft is in the background.

aircraft rather than eject, that is preferable, but these rules-of-thumb help in a pinch.

FORMAL BRIEF

The day begins with a formal brief in the flight room. The first thing students do is make sure that the room is arranged for the brief and "standup" that follows each

morning. Students sit in a circle, in front of their IP. The flight leader calls the room to attention when the flight commander enters, declaring, "Sir, Eagle Flight all present and accounted for." The flight commander responds, "Turn and greet your IPs." Students then salute the IPs, and are commanded to take their seats. They sit with feet flat on the floor, heels together. The brief starts with students briefing on the previously researched weather for the day, runway use, traffic patterns, and other information necessary for a day of safe flight.

Next come notes, warnings, and cautions. These have to be memorized word for word. Each day they are different, and they take several hours to memorize beforehand. The instructors call on each student to give the note, warning, or caution for the assigned reading. After this come the shotgun questions, which concern the assigned reading of the night before, and every student has to correctly answer one of these questions. Students stand at attention as one-by-one the instructor asks each question. They sit down if they get it

Above: An IP and student pilot of the Third Flying Training Squadron conduct a preflight inspection on a T-6A Texan II.

An IP climbs into a T-37 while a student does the preflight before a training flight.

A T-6A Texan II flies side by side with a World War II–vintage AT-6 Texan. Civilian military aviation enthusiasts still fly many vintage AT-6s.

Below: An IP inspects the rotator blades on a T-6A Texan II before a JSUPT sortie.

right, and remain standing if they get it wrong. The IP comes back to the students who are still standing for another round of questions. Students keep standing until they answer a question correctly. A student who says they do not know an answer will end up with the "bone," a big plastic bone they must carry with them for a week.

The last, most difficult, and perhaps most important item in the formal brief is the emergency procedure, or the EP standup. An IP takes the platform and randomly calls on a student, who must come to attention. Every student must begin the EP saying, "I will maintain aircraft control, analyze the situation, and take appropriate action, and land as soon as conditions permit."

Students had better not miss questions early in the briefs. They only become more difficult later. Any items that appear in boldface on the aircraft checklist must be recited word for word. If students miss any of these in the first stage of EP training, they are admonished. As training progresses from low-level threats to more serious situations, students must solve more complex emergencies. If a student makes an error at this point, they may get a "sit-down," which means being barred from a flight that day.

The EP covers the initial encounter with the emergency, and whether ejection or emergency landing is the necessary course of action. The IP teaches students real-world emergency procedures. For most stand-ups, the students are given the premise that they are solo with no IP in the cockpit. For example, the airplane is flying at

The T-6A Texan II performs a "gear-down" pass. The Texan II is now replacing the aging T-37 fleet.

100 KIAS, has 18 degrees of flaps deployed, and is climbing through 3,000 feet AGL with the throttle in the full-power position. The engine is losing power, and the RPMs are approaching idle. The IP asks students what course of action they would recommend.

First, students ask the IP questions about the weather, airport environment, any anomalies in the "engine-start" checklist, or any questions they feel are appropriate and necessary to analyze the EP. Then students go into painstaking, detailed responses to resolve the emergency.

The EPs emphasize the most important factor in an emergency—control of the aircraft. After students have completed their analysis, they take control of the situation and do whatever has to be done to safely resolve the emergency. For example, in the case of possible engine failure of a single-engine T-6A, they might establish the best glide path for a safe landing, while maintaining separation from other traffic on or near the runway. Students are taught to take the time to examine the options, make a decision, and perform the right action.

DOLLAR RIDE

A student's first ride with the IP is jokingly called the "dollar ride," in reference to the dollar tip the student gives the IP for the ride. Students usually decorate the bills with drawings or other embellishments, and the IPs may display them on their desks.

The ride starts with the mandatory exercise for every flight a pilot will ever make, the preflight "walkaround." Students use a predetermined written checklist and walk around the aircraft, inspecting the external parts of the airplane. They check tires for pressure and wear and examine the flight controls (flaps, ailerons, rudder, and elevator) to make sure they move freely, do not feel binding, and do not chafe along other surfaces. They check that the access panels are secure, that oil and hydraulic fluid levels are correct, and that the pitot (pronounced "peeto") tube, which measures airspeed, is clear of debris. Students inspect the fuselage, static port, and propeller for visible damage, or, if it is a jet-propelled trainer, they check the jet intakes for debris. Although not prescribed but often done by the pilot,

A head-on view of the T-6A Texan II.

they may run their hand along the leading edge of the wings or other parts of the fuselage, checking for structural integrity or simply to make a connection with their machine.

Once the student completes the walk-around, they climb into the cockpit, and then begin the before-start checklist by reporting to their instructor: "Sir, I have two leg, two shoulder, one chest, lap belt, silver key, zero-delay lanyard connect. . . ." The silver key, part of the five-point harness assembly, is a small metal device that connects directly to the parachute. In case of ejection, this key allows for automatic parachute opening immediately after the pilot is "kicked" from their seat, otherwise called "man-seat separation." If the automatic opening system senses an outside altitude greater than between 11,500 and 15,000 feet, it will delay opening (meaning the pilot will fall face down with the seat on their back) until within that block. The time interval between pulling the handles to full chute is a mere 3.42 seconds. The zero-delay lanyard is used only in the T-37, and then only below 10,000 feet. It is connected by the pilot directly to the "D" handle used for pulling the parachute ripcord. It reduces by a fraction of a second the amount of time it takes to deploy the parachute, thus giving the aircrew a slightly larger margin for getting a full chute before hitting the ground.

The checklist encourages repetition. If a pilot performs the same task repeatedly, it should become so automatic that they will not make mistakes. Certain

Student and IP taxi out in a T-38A trainer for a lesson.

The Air Force has a proud heritage of enlisted aviators. During World War II, candidates had to have a high school diploma, rate in the top 50 percent of their high school class, have at least 1.5 credits in math, and be between the ages of 18 and 22. About 4,150 pilots trained and flew as enlisted men. Out of their ranks came 17 aces and 11 generals, and more than 155 were killed in action. Retired Brigadier General Chuck Yeager was one of those enlisted pilots.

Charles E. "Chuck" Yeager

IPs often compare notes on the progress of their students.

The T-33 Shooting Star (also called the T-Bird) was the Air Force's first jet trainer. The two-seat T-33 was developed from the first operational jet fighter, the Lockheed F-80 Shooting Star, a single-seat fighter. This T-33 now stands silent watch as a "Gate Guard." *Henry M. Holden*

items on the checklist require challenge and response; the student reads off those items to the IP, who gives a reply. However, most checklist training is intended to teach students to do things on their own. The IP does not act as a copilot, but rather as a safety observer, since the students are being trained to act as aircraft commanders (AC) for their eventual solo flights.

In one scenario, a student might say to the IP, "Sir, I have one crew chief, one fire bottle, no oxygen or refueling within 50 feet, clear fore, aft, and left, and you?" The student in this example cannot see any objects that might be on the right side of the T-37.

"Clear on the right," the IP replies.

After the before-start checklist is complete and the student and IP are strapped in, the student begins the engine-start checklist by lighting the first engine. Once the engine spools up and the gauges come alive, they light the second engine to complete the checklist. The student will then go through the after-start checklist, making sure the generators are on line, the engine anti-icing is set properly, and so forth. Clearance for taxi is requested after engines are started, and all systems are checked. At JSUPT bases, contrary to most civilian airfields, a clearance for engine start is not required. The student climbs in, runs

through the appropriate checklists, starts the engines, and requests taxi clearance.

"Sir, after-start checklist is complete."

TAKEOFF

The student or IP requests permission from ground control to taxi, and the IP taxis to the active runway. Except for the first few rides, the student does all the taxiing. A ground controller clears them to follow specific taxiways that lead to the active runway, where they "hold short" for the controller's instructions to enter the runway. There a pre-takeoff checklist is completed. For the T-37, they commit the following catchphrase to memory: "Hook, look, wiggle, jiggle, two-one-two, review." It will cover such things as double-checking proper strap-in procedures, free and correct movement of the flight controls, turning on exterior lights, and ensuring selection of the proper frequency for takeoff.

"Sheppard Tower, Cider twenty-six, number one, fifteen left," the student radios the controller.

"Cider twenty-six, cleared for takeoff runway fifteen left," the controller replies.

"Cleared for takeoff fifteen left, Cider twenty-six"

The IP and student will visually check for incoming

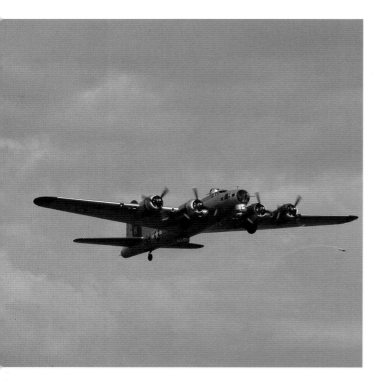

As the aircraft accelerates, the flight controls slowly become active and the airplane begins to perform as it was designed. The thrust of the engine, plus the shape of the wings, air temperature, and weight will enable the aircraft to lift off the ground at a predetermined speed. The Bernoulli principle states that as air rushes over the curved top of the wing and under the flat bottom of the wing, the faster-moving air on top of the wing creates a pressure differential. Since the pressure is greater beneath the wing, it will exert upward pressure, or lift, on the wing.

At nose wheel liftoff (NWLO) speed, the nose wheel will lift off the ground. However, the aircraft is not necessarily ready to fly, since there may be insufficient lift. At takeoff speed, there is finally enough lift to fly, and the main wheels lift off the ground. Typically, there is a 20-30 knot difference between NWLO and takeoff speed.

In the preflight briefing, students have also worked out takeoff and landing data (TOLD) to determine if there is a mechanical malfunction. Before every flight, TOLD is calculated from performance charts based on the current temperature and winds. Typically, this is discussed in terms of "go/no-go" speeds. At go speed, also called "decision" speed, the pilot can lose an engine and still accelerate and take off in the remaining runway on one engine. No-go speed, also called "refusal" or "abort" speed, is the fastest speed at which a pilot can take a plane with enough runway to bring the aircraft to a complete stop in case of malfunction. For any problems beyond no-go speed, the pilot must take the aircraft into the air. This sometimes means continuing a takeoff with only one good engine.

More than 10,000 B-17s were built during World War II. Only a handful still survives. *Henry M. Holden*

traffic before entering the runway. Then the IP moves the throttle levers forward, increases the RPMs, ensures proper limits for the engine instruments to include oil and hydraulic pressure, releases the foot brakes, and begins the takeoff roll. The student watches the airspeed indicator ensuring acceleration on two good engines.

In 1976, the Air Force admitted women to flight training. However, during World War II, a civilian group called the Women Airforce Service Pilots (WASPs) flew every transport, bomber, and fighter in the Army Air Force inventory. Head of the WASPs was Jacqueline Cochran, a close personal friend of Amelia Earhart and, later, test pilot Captain Chuck Yeager. Although civilians, the WASPs were subject to military training and discipline. They were essentially test pilots, since they flew the airplanes as they rolled off the assembly line, untested. The WASPs delivered 12,650 planes of 77 different types and flew half of all high-speed pursuit planes ferried in the United States. More than 25,000 women applied to be WASPs, and of the 1,830 women admitted, 1,074 graduated. They flew more than 60 million miles, and 38 lost their lives in accidents and in operations. In 1976, the WASPs petitioned Congress for recognition, and on November 23, 1977, President Jimmy Carter signed the WASP Bill, more than 30 years after the WASPs disbanded. Official acceptance into the Air Force came in 1979.

An F-16 shoots an air-to-air missile.

The T-37 takeoff and landing rolls are so short—given little more than a 6,000-foot runway—that if the abort decision is made, the troubled aircraft may actually be in the air yet still be able to land, as long as the gear is still down. For example, any malfunctions below refusal speed are cause for aborting the takeoff. If the pilot experiences any malfunctions after refusal speed, they will continue the takeoff. The IP will advise ATC that there is a problem and that they need to fly the runway heading (straight ahead after takeoff) at 1,500 feet or safe altitude so ATC can adjust the traffic accordingly. Once at a safe altitude, the IP will stabilize the airplane, retract the flaps, and analyze the situation. Until the pilot determines what is wrong, they will not declare an emergency. If there is an electrical malfunction, for example, the pilot will first check the DC-voltmeter to see if the battery is still charging and go through the appropriate checklist. Only then may the pilot declare an emergency and request an immediate vector back to base.

Except for the first one or two rides, during takeoffs the student calls out certain speeds, simply for the development of good habit patterns, since ultimately they have

PILOT TRAINING IN WORLD WAR II

One of the greatest accomplishments of the U.S. Army Air Forces (AAF) in World War II was training hundreds of thousands of flying and ground personnel for the war. Coming from all lifestyles, they were molded into the most formidable air force the world had ever seen. Primary flight schools operated by civilian companies provided basic and advanced flight training for the AAF. The civilian schools used Stearman, Ryan, and Fairchild trainers owned by the AAF. Each cadet received 60 hours of flight training in nine weeks before attending basic flight school.

During basic flight training, a cadet received approximately 70 hours in the air during a nine-week period. The basic course made military pilots of those who had learned only the fundamentals of flight in primary school. In addition to flying an airplane of greater weight, horsepower, and speed such as the BT-9 or BT-13, cadets learned how to fly at night, on instruments, in formation, and cross country. For the first time, pilots were operating planes equipped with a two-way radio and a two-pitch propeller. From this point, cadets would move on to either single-engine or twin-engine advanced flying school.

Cadets at single-engine school flew AT-6 Texans for 70 hours during a nine-week period, learning aerial gunnery and combat maneuvers, and

During World War II, the Boeing Stearman PT-17 was used as a trainer before students stepped up to the AT-6 Texan. *Henry M. Holden*

increasing their skills in navigation, formation flying, and instrument flying.

Cadets assigned to twin-engine school received the same number of flying hours but did not practice combat aerobatics or gunnery. Instead, they honed their ability to fly on instruments—at night and in formation—after first mastering the art of flying a plane with more than one engine. The Curtiss AT-9 "Jeep" and the Beech AT-10 "Wichita" were among the advanced trainer aircraft used to transition between single-engine trainers and twin-engine combat aircraft.

Those who graduated were usually assigned to transition training in the type of plane they would fly in combat. Some were assigned to specific squadrons already scheduled for overseas duty. Others were assigned to replacement training units for subsequent assignment to squadrons already overseas. Regardless, a pilot required two months of additional training before they were considered ready for combat.

Even after completing all their training, pilots perished before they saw combat. Second Lieutenant Joseph Barradi was a new B-17 pilot who headed for England in his brand new bomber. "We had a flight of about 50 airplanes," he said. "Just before I left, a pilot who had just returned from England took me aside. He told me if the weather got bad (and it was always bad during the winter in the North Atlantic), remember to keep the trailing wire antenna extended, and fly as low as possible to the water. He said that the antenna would be the only connection with the other airplanes. The weather was bad most of the trip, and most of us lost contract with each other. I flew about 100 feet above the waves for almost six hours before the weather cleared, and we saw the coast of England. When we landed, we counted 42 airplanes. Eight planes just disappeared somewhere in the Atlantic. That was 80 men gone before anybody took a shot at us.".

to execute these habits when they go solo. Once airborne, the student covers the after-takeoff checklist: gear up at 100 KIAS (minimum), flaps up, and so on.

"Sir, gear clear."

"Gear clear," the IP repeats, and the student retracts the landing gear. An audible thump can be heard in the cockpit as the gear retracts.

It is important to repeat checklist commands to make sure the pilot hears the correct command. Since students will eventually take the aircraft solo, the repetition of checklist items is more to develop good individual habits rather than emphasizing crew resource management (CRM). Although CRM is a secondary focus, and even though there are some challenge-and-response items on the checklist, good checklist discipline is necessary so that students can successfully execute all required items on solo flights.

With the wheels and flaps retracted, the airframe is "clean," and the airplane gains speed. If the IP made the takeoff, they may now hand the controls over to the student, who would then fly to an auxiliary airfield where traffic is light.

The IP demonstrates a straight-in pattern and landing, as well as several "overhead" patterns and landing, and allows the student to make two of them. The landing itself is quite different from one in a Cessna 150. The Tweet makes a steep approach on final.

The "overhead and closed downwind" patterns differ drastically from the rectangular pattern the student previously flew for their PPC. This is a tactical maneuver whereby the pilot flies up "initial," directly over the approach end of the runway of intended landing at anywhere from 1,000 to 10,000 feet, then executes an aggressive 3–5 G, 180-degree "break" in which the pilot slows the aircraft in preparation for lowering the gear and flaps. After completing the 180-degree turn, the pilot is momentarily on "closed downwind," now parallel to the runway but offset by about 3,000 to 5,000 feet. Depending on altitude, the higher the initial, the closer the offset to the runway. Almost immediately after rolling out on closed downwind, the pilot hits the "perch."

At the perch, the student ensures that their gear and flaps are down and initiates a diving, continuous 180-degree turn to line up on an approximately one-and-a-quarter-mile final approach, on about a 3-degree glidepath. The student then flies the aircraft down, rolling out on about a 1-NM final approach while slowing to final approach speed in preparation for his flare

Above: A U.S. Air Force F-16C Fighting Falcon aircraft from the 148th Fighter Wing, Minnesota Air National Guard, flies a combat air patrol mission over the Eastern Seaboard of the United States in support of Operation Noble Eagle.

Right: The C-141 Starlifter was the first pure jet designed for transporting cargo. Its 93-foot-long cargo bay can hold up to 208 ground troops or 168 paratroops. It has a wingspan of 160 feet; is 168 feet, 4 inches long; 39 feet, 3 inches high; and has a ceiling of 41,000 feet.

A C-141 Starlifter disgorges its paratroops.

to touch down on the first 500 – 1,000 feet of runway. The overhead pattern is exactly what these student pilots will fly when and if they graduate and move on to larger, faster aircraft.

In a combat environment, this way of getting the aircraft on the ground quickly keeps the amount of time aircrew are exposed to short-range ground-to-air threats to an absolute minimum. In JSUPT, they teach the overhead pattern in lieu of the rectangular pattern since they need to accomplish more patterns in a short amount of time.

The aircraft is then cleared into a military operations area (MOA) airspace, and the student is permitted to do various maneuvers such as loops and aileron rolls (i.e., rolling the airplane over quickly) to get the feel for the airplane and pull some Gs. This first ride is more relaxed and informal since the student is not being graded on their performance. However, within a month of the dollar ride, the student will face the pressure of having to fly solo.

THREE

Solo to
Silver Wings

In preparation for their solo flight, the student begins with basic area work, straight and level flight, turns, glides, and slow flight. They also practice stalls, spin recovery, lazy eights, abnormal flight recoveries (inverted, nose high, and nose low), and chandelles. A chandelle is a maximum-performance climbing turn that results in a 180-degree change in direction. It is a fast way to change direction and climb quickly.

By now, the pressure for these students to perform is at an unprecedented level. With less than a handful of military flying hours in their logbook, the IPs are keeping score and evaluating students on every specific action—or inaction—on every flight.

Each flight brings new challenges for the students as IPs up the ante. It is no longer acceptable to fly off altitude or too fast, with very little room for error. For example, up to 200 feet off altitude or 20 KIAS off speed must be swiftly corrected to the desired parameters. For now, it is not about how students fly; it is about knowing where the airplane is supposed to be, at what speed, and making the appropriate corrections to get there. If at this stage a particular student knows what they are supposed to be doing, but has not yet developed all the necessary skills to do so,

An air-to-air view shows the IP's position onboard a T-38 Talon aircraft from the 560th Flying Training Squadron, Randolph Air Force Base, Texas. The IP is watching his wingman flying in formation.

that is far better than not knowing what the power setting, altitude, and speed should be. As the solo ride draws ever closer, the mental pressure on the student becomes more and more intense.

The 12-hour days are capped off by three hours of evening study, and then the student grabs some sleep before doing it all over again the next day. The IPs are no longer talking the student through procedures or maneuvers—they better have it down cold on terra firma if they hope to be up to the task in the air. At this point, some students begin to realize that a pilot's job is not for them. It takes serious motivation and a clear vision to continue. This is when students begin to "wash out," or what is known as self-induced elimination (SIE).

Training is accelerating, and tasks are becoming harder for some to master. Recovery from stalls and spins takes coordination, practice, and for many students, a strong stomach. At 20,000 feet, the IP stalls the airplane

In December 2001, Second Lieutenant Kimberly Krohmer was the first student—and the first female—to solo in the Air Force's newest trainer, the T-6 Texan II.

by pulling the nose up until the wings no longer have lift. Then they kick in full rudder, and the airplane starts spinning downward. The nose drops 40 to 45 degrees below the horizon; the airplane is spinning about one turn every three seconds, dropping 550 feet with each turn. The IP will demonstrates the recovery and brings the airplane back to controlled flight. Students then practice until they master the recovery.

When the IP decides that the student has mastered all the lessons and is safe to fly, they let the student land,

A Royal Netherlands Air Force cadet goes through the traditional dunking after his initial solo flight. The cadet is one of approximately 320 students taking part in the 80th Flying Training Wing's Euro-NATO joint jet pilot training program.

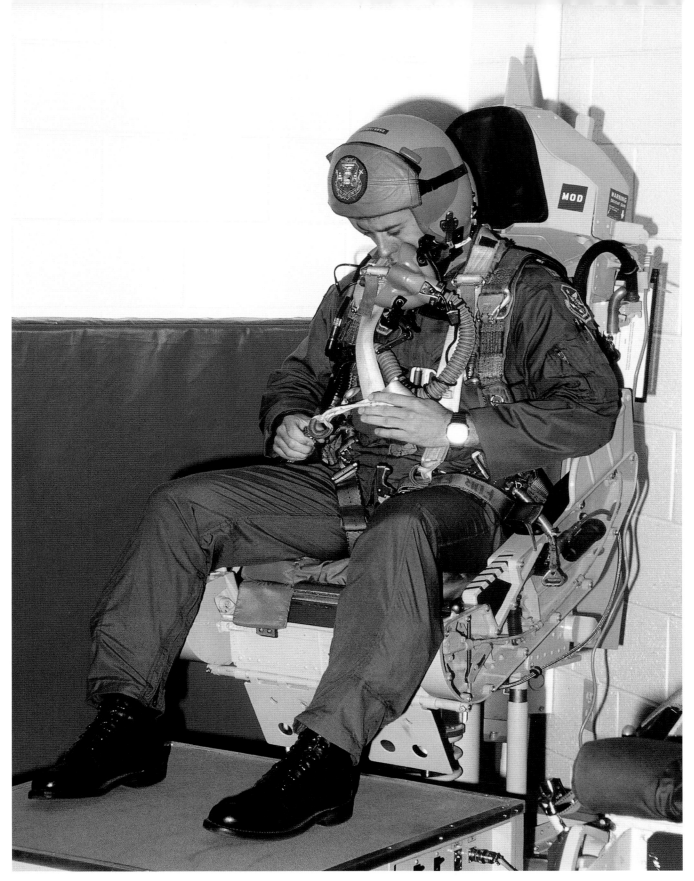

A pilot checks his harness on an ejection seat simulator.

and taxi back to the chocks. Then they lend the student their nametag with wings and send them into the sky—alone. Since the student does not yet have their own wings, the instructor's wings are "flying" with them on their initial solo. At this point, the student picks up a temporary call sign. It may be "Scare," or "Wings," common call signs for initial solo students.

At first, the student is a little anxious. But once they accomplish their first takeoff and they realize they are flying—alone—they start to gain confidence. They will fly around the pattern, and report to ATC, "Wings twelve, request touch and go." The ATC clears them to a specific runway, and on their approach they check their flap setting, RPMs, and more, while scanning the sky for traffic and maintaining proper displacement from the runway. They do three "touch and goes," landing the wheels on the runway, and without stopping, reset trim, set flaps 18 degrees to ensure a positive climb rate, apply power, maintain slight forward pressure on the control column to keep the nose from rising until proper airspeed is established, then apply slight back pressure to the control column. The airplane will break ground, and climb. The student will "clean up the airplane" (retract the gear and flaps) and follow the predetermined departure pattern.

Another tradition associated with a student's initial solo flight is the traditional "dunking," in which the student is tossed into a tank of water after their initial solo. When the student gets back on the ground, the class tackles him and throws him in the solo dunk tank. If they do not catch the student and the student makes it back to the flight room, the class owes the student a beverage of their choice. That almost never happens, since the whole class of 15 to 20 students is chasing one student, and there is only one open door into the building.

Students display a noticeable change after their first solo. They have more confidence, and a little swagger in their walk, but they are still a long way from their silver wings.

After their initial solo, the students will start double turning, meaning they will fly two flights in one day. Before this, they flew one flight and one simulator ride each day. One ride in the next seven after the initial solo is a pattern-only flight, where the student flies solo around the base and lands. With each student, the IP decides if it is safe for them to leave the base and fly to the MOA alone as practice. At this point, the students begin to feel like pilots. They can sign out on the aircraft, strap it on, light the engines, and fly away, alone.

After they land and taxi back, if the jet is broken or needs maintenance, it must be taken off the flying schedule and the student calls in a "Code 3" to the duty desk. If the student is with an IP, the IP will call the codes. In an operational squadron, the pilot will call in the codes to the duty desk after every sortie. Code 1 means the jet is good to go, and can fly again that same day. Code 2 means the jet needs minor maintenance that could probably be accomplished before its next flight that same day.

MID-PHASE CHECKRIDE

The mid-phase checkride is the first of four checkrides that students take. This requires intensive preparation, and has the highest failure rate, with a 55 percent pass rate. The mid-phase checkride measures the student's basic flying skills, area orientation (staying in the proper block of airspace in the MOA), and general knowledge of local procedures and aircraft systems.

Now it becomes survival of the fittest. If a student fails three consecutive sorties before a checkride, they go before a Commanders Review Board (CRB), which decides if they should stay in the program. Moreover, if a student fails a checkride, and then fails two more follow-up rides, or if they fail three academic tests during JSUPT (including ground school), they must face a CRB.

At this point, students are learning how to perform almost every aerobatic maneuver in the book: loops, aileron and barrel rolls, Immelmann, cloverleafs, Cuban eights, and the Split S used in a dogfight to pull down and get on the enemy's "six." Students practice them in the MOA, and they are also learning to fly on instruments. The experience is very different from the simulator. In the air, the inner ear tries to trick students. What is "up" may not be. Students may think they are in a bank, but are not. The training continues, and students learn to trust the instruments, or they will wash out.

CROSS-COUNTRY TRAINING

Before students earn their wings, they must navigate and fly hundreds of miles from a base, land at military fields, and return. Students fly both in daylight and at night. This will also involve flying with the big boys in the Class A airspace, which ranges from 18,000 feet mean sea level (MSL) to 60,000 feet (also called FL600). All operations in this airspace must be under instrument flight rules (IFR), and are subject to ATC clearances and instructions. The cross-country flight is used to give students an idea of what the national air traffic system is, and how the pieces come together.

The world is divided into 25 time zones, 23 of which span 15 degrees of longitude; the remaining two divide a single 15-degree section (politics and geography affect the precise boundaries). Time zones are numbered from -12 through 0 to +12, indicating their difference in hours compared to Greenwich Mean Time (GMT). GMT is centered on the prime meridian—zero longitude—which runs through Greenwich, England. On the opposite side of the world from Greenwich, 180 degrees away, the International Date Line separates the remaining 15-degree section into +12 to the west and -12 to the east. Civilian time zone designations are typically three-letter abbreviations such as EST (Eastern Standard Time). Military and aviation designations use the military alphabet code (except J), such as Zulu (GMT).

This flight takes students and IPs to McGuire Air Reserve Base in New Jersey. The student tunes the radio to the automated terminal information service (ATIS). "McGuire arrival information Yankee." The latest airport briefing conditions are known as "Yankee."

"Two-one-zero-zero Zulu weather [note: Zulu is military time based on Greenwich Mean Time]. One four thousand scattered [clouds]."

"Visibility, one five [miles]. Temperature, seven five. Dew point, five-one [amount of moisture in the air]. Wind two-seven-five [degrees], at one-five [knots]." Tonight the weather is perfect. But before students earn their wings, they will make cross-country flights in less than perfect weather. It is all part of becoming a U.S. Air Force pilot.

Flying in a four-ship formation of F-16s armed with deadly ordnance is possible only through hours of practice.

FORMATION FLYING

Formation flying is fundamental to Air Force pilot training and is used to teach aggressiveness. A student cannot stay in a good flight position with another airplane unless they are aggressive. On their solo formation flight, the student is constantly aware that they must not make contact with the other jet. Until the formation solo, the student knows in the back of their mind that they can make mistakes, because the IP is there to back them up if they get into trouble.

Most pilots love the challenge of flying 3 feet from the wing of the next airplane. One maneuver students learn is called "offset trail." Two jets are on the same power setting, one is leading, and the other follows (in trail) through all the banks and turns. The student uses different pursuit angles to stay with the leader. The student is 300 to 500 feet behind the leader the whole time, unless they call "blind." That is when the wingman loses sight of the leader. If the flight leader loses their wingman, they may also call blind, or in most cases simply call for

their wingman's "posit" or position in relation to the lead aircraft. It is the basics of dogfighting.

In formation flying, students are graded not only on how well they fly the wing, but also on how well they lead. Leading is harder to fly than wing position. As lead, a student has to be smooth and predictable for the wingman, and the lead has to keep the formation in the area. Leading is harder, because if the student is approaching the practice area borders, they cannot just whip the jet around, or they will lose their wingman. The student has to plan about five or six steps ahead, based on where they are in the area, what their energy level is, and what else they need to give their wingman. The energy level is a combination of the aircraft's altitude and airspeed. A certain airspeed is needed to have Gs available to do some of the maneuvers, and minimum speeds are associated with some maneuvers.

Students also make two low-level formation flights at 500 feet on a military training route. On this type of flight, the student is flying to points on the ground and timing

A pilot maneuvers his B-52 Stratofortress into position beneath a KC-135 Stratotanker for aerial refueling. Aerial refueling is a precision dance that comes only from hours of practicing this special-formation flying. It takes steady hands, as the two jets are traveling just yards apart at 300 to 400 miles per hour in turbulent skies.

The tail codes of these T-38s training in a four-ship formation indicate they are from Columbus Air Force Base.

the points. The end purpose is to arrive at the target at the end of the route, on time. This involves recognizing different landmarks and adjusting airspeed to get there.

By flying the T-6A and the Tweet, students have learned the basic skills needed to progress to one of four advanced training tracks: bomber/fighter, airlift/tanker, turboprop, or helicopter.

TRACK SELECT

Those students who have survived the first six months of 12-hour days and have managed to memorize the thousands of aircraft specifications and performance charts have made it to the halfway point in JSUPT. Now students will be funneled into one of four advanced training tracks based on class standing. Students submit their choices in order of preference, and, depending on what slots are available and how well they did in primary training, they may get their first choice, or they may get another choice.

For example, there may be 26 students in a class. The class "drop" includes perhaps nine T-38 slots for the fighter/bomber track, 13 T-1A spots for the airlift/tanker track, three T-44 slots for the turboprop track, and one helicopter slot. Generally, IPs try to give everyone their first choice, depending on availability, but IPs have the final say on who goes where. For instance, if fighter spots are still open by the time someone in the bottom 25 percent of the class is selected, and the flight commander determines that the person is not qualified to fly fighters, that person will get another assignment, such as the T-1 or T-44.

Each of the four tracks has different follow-up training in

A 39th Flying Training Squadron IP goes over evasive maneuvers with an IFF (Introduction to Fighter Fundamentals) student pilot during a pre-mission brief.

75

An IP from the 25th Flying Training Squadron observes a student pilot perform a preflight inspection on a T-38 Talon.

the type of aircraft that students will be flying. Two factors go into determining track selection: instructor inputs by way of officer evaluations and student input. For example, not every student can go to advanced fighter training in the F-15E Strike Eagle. Only the best basic pilots are picked for this training. The instructors decide which aircraft are assigned to which students by

Of the 71,442 officers in the U. S. Air Force, 12,714 are pilots. The majority fall into three categories: fighter pilots, 3,200; airlift pilots, 3,000; and IP, 1,400. Currently, about 464, or 3.7 percent, of all pilots are female.

putting their grades in a computer that calculates a rank order. The number-one student gets to pick the aircraft they want to fly.

Surviving the first half of JSUPT is a milestone, but the worst is yet to come. The pressure will continue to increase, with the student learning thousands of new facts and aircraft performance stats about the next training aircraft he will fly. Testing, checkrides, and grading continue unabated, allowing only the most highly motivated and best skilled to succeed.

THE FUGE

Every student rides the centrifuge, or fuge, which is a gondola-like capsule at the end of a long arm. The inside of the fuge resembles an aircraft cockpit, with a control column and a heads-up display (HUD). An engine turns the arm, which rotates the gondola. As the rotations increase

A student pilot (front) and his instructor fly in formation during a T-38C Talon training flight.

in speed, the transverse inertial force on the student is the same as a pilot experiences in a high-G maneuver. The short, tiring, and unpleasant ride serves as an introduction to the high-G environment of a jet fighter pilot. A camera records the student's physiological reactions for later debriefing with the instructor.

Humans normally move at 3 to 4 miles per hour under 1 G of gravity on the ground. The body does not deal well with the high Gs often experienced in jet fighter aircraft. G-force is directly related to only two factors: airspeed and turn radius. When a modern fighter jet performs aerobatic maneuvers, it can create a force equivalent to over eight times the pilot's weight, or 8 Gs.

The Air Force flew an average of 300 strike sorties a day the first week of Operation Iraqi Freedom. To fly that many combat missions, pilots relied on Air Force tanker aircraft to keep their planes juiced. Army and marine ground units moved so fast that fighters didn't have enough time to return from Saudi Arabia, over which the tankers were flying, to south of Baghdad to destroy Iraqi forces before the American ground units advanced. Commanders made the bold decision to move tankers over Iraq so the fighters could fuel up and return to battle more quickly. The Iraqis fired at the lumbering tanker aircraft with both artillery and surface-to-air missiles. The commanders were willing to risk a tanker and its crew to get the fighters to Baghdad and protect the fast-moving ground forces. The pilots flew the vulnerable tanker aircraft with no radar-warning equipment, chaff, or flares to divert the missiles. The commanders expected to lose at least one tanker, but none were hit.

Above: This view of the interior of a Dynamic Environment Simulator at Wright-Patterson Air Force Base, Ohio, shows a study subject in place.

Left: An officer is strapped into the cab of the centrifuge at Wright-Patterson Air Force Base, Ohio.

Gravity is constantly pulling all objects toward the center of the earth. As a pilot maneuvers an aircraft, the "pull" force of gravity multiplies, since inertial force is acting on the aircraft and its crew. Another way of looking at the force of gravity is not as a hand pushing a pilot down in their seat, but as a hand trying to pull him through the bottom of their seat. Since the seat does not give way, and since human bodies are sensitive to the effects of gravity, the pilot feels an increased pull force when they try to turn an airplane around a very tight turn. The effects of this equivalent extra weight on the human body are far-reaching. Since the pilot's equivalent weight has increased, the heart has to work harder to pump blood, and the diaphragm has to work harder to ensure that they keep on breathing. Blood is drawn away from their brain, and pools in the lower portions of the body. At higher G-levels, pilots can lose consciousness from a lack of blood and oxygen to the brain. The stress on the body becomes so great that the brain shuts down in an attempt to save itself. This effect is known as G-induced

The Introduction to Fighter Fundamentals course uses the T-38C Talon. The extension from the nose of the airplane is the pitot tube.

loss of consciousness (G-LOC). The first symptoms of G-LOC are graying vision and then tunnel vision, in which the rods in the eyes start to lose blood.

The T-37 Tweet has the highest G onset rate of any airplane in the Air Force. This means that a student can go from zero to 6 Gs in half a second. G-LOC occurs after the five or six seconds worth of oxygen stored in the brain is depleted. To prevent this, students are taught, within the safety of the fuge, to perform an anti-G-strain maneuver (AGSM) before the onset of G-LOC, to resist the G-forces acting on their bodies.

Students wear special G-suits, but the suits only help increase the pilot's tolerance by about 1 G. As Gs increase, the G-suit inflates bladders in the legs and lower body, forcing the blood to remain in the upper part of the body and the brain. To provide the bridge to 8 or 9 Gs, students practice the AGSM before stepping into the fuge.

The AGSM involves flexing the skeletal muscles—mostly legs and buttocks—and doing cyclic breathing to keep the lungs full. Students try to exhale against a closed glottis in their throat. This helps keep blood pumping to the brain, but it is an unnatural, demanding, and tiring

IPs take their students on a formation training flight in the T-38C Talon.

An IP checks flight instruments in his T-38C Talon before departing on a training sortie with a pilot trainee. The T-38C has significant enhancements over previous models, including GPS, a ring-laser gyro inertial navigation system, radar altimeter, traffic collision avoidance system, and an instrument-flight-certified heads-up display.

activity. The students continue to practice AGSM until it becomes second nature, and are critiqued on their performance, but not graded. Grading comes later for the students going on to fighter school.

FIGHTER TRACK

For students moving to the F-15C, F-15E, F-16, and the A-10, the T-38 Talon is the perfect transitional aircraft. It is fast, agile, and has tandem seating. In theory, the Air Force teaches the basic principles that apply to all fighter

aircraft in a more economical aircraft — the T-38C Talon II. The T-38C costs one-third less per flying hour to operate than an F-16, and one-fifth less per hour than an F-15.

Instructors gradually turn their students into the best fighter pilots in the world by demonstrating techniques and then watching the students replicate every move. The instructor must identify the student's weaknesses, and help turn them into strengths. The pressure to perform is on, and every ride feels like a checkride. One word continually pops up—*speed*—which is exemplified

Two pilots of the 149th Fighter Wing, Texas Air National Guard, Kelly Air Force Base, Texas, wear the new Libelle anti-gravity flight suit that should improve a pilot's ability to handle the latest generation of high-performance jet aircraft. Anti-G suits help prevent a pilot from losing consciousness during rapid acceleration or tight turns in aircraft like the F-15E Strike Eagle. The Libelle is a liquid-filled, full-body, anti-G suit that promises advantages over the pneumatic anti-G suits currently in use.

An IP does a walk-around on a T-38 Talon.

by the T-38. It is when the instructor sits in tandem with the student in the aircraft to help troubleshoot in case of confusion that the real learning takes place. But it does not stop there. After every flight, instructors debrief the students and break down every aspect of the mission. The next flight should go more smoothly.

Still, fighter pilot training is not for everyone. If a student can't hack it sortie after sortie for the whole duration, they are not destined to be a U.S. Air Force fighter pilot.

Because of the nature of fighter aircraft and missions, the top JSUPT students generally put in for the T-38 Talon II, unless they put in for the T-1A. This would open a slot down the list for another pilot who might otherwise not be slotted for the T-38.

The T-38 is also the transitional aircraft for bomber pilots. Whether they fly the B-1, B-2, or B-52 bomber, they will spend six grueling months under the hot Texas sun mastering the T-38. This is where the instructors put the final touches on promising students, and perhaps soon-to-be Air Force pilots.

AIRLIFT AND TANKER TRACK

Flying a tanker or cargo aircraft may not attract the same attention as flying a sleek fighter aircraft, but the students who fly them become a vital link in transport and special operations missions, and their jobs are no less dangerous.

The T-1A Jayhawk is a modified business jet, and instruments are the heart and soul of this training jet. Students must have a solid base in the procedures, and be able to fly and do instrument navigation anywhere in the world. T-1A students must learn to work with a crew and be good copilots and, eventually, aircraft commanders.

81

They are introduced to crew resource management techniques, air-to-air refueling, airdrop missions, radar positioning, and navigation. This is where students learn that making mistakes is not always a bad thing. They learn from them and move on.

Prospective airlift tanker pilots complete their training in the T-1A Jayhawk, a medium-range, twin-engine jet trainer. Students in this track go on to fly the Air Force heavyweights, cargo aircraft such as C-5s, C-17s, C-130s, the Reserve C-141, or KC-135 and KC-10 refueling aircraft. Students assigned to the airlift/tanker track are trained at Columbus Air Force Base, Mississippi; Laughlin Air Force Base, Texas; or Vance Air Force Base, Oklahoma.

Long before students get into the cockpit of a T-1A Jayhawk, they spend a month in the classroom learning every switch, button, and system. Students learn quickly that planning is one of the most important parts of the mission, and they also learn that it can be tedious. Every facet of the flight is planned and discussed in detail. Students must be prepared for anything as the lessons get longer and more difficult. There are at least four simulator sessions, each about six hours long, before students fly the training aircraft. This is where CRM is put into practice, where two pilots learn to work as a team in the cockpit. Here the pilot is introduced to flying with a copilot, with whom they spend the rest of the training.

Above: A second lieutenant looks over her shoulder during a preflight check of the T-1A aircraft. With her is an IP from the 14th Flying Training Wing. This lieutenant was the first female to enter the T-1A training program.

Left: A backwards view from a climbing T-37 Tweet.

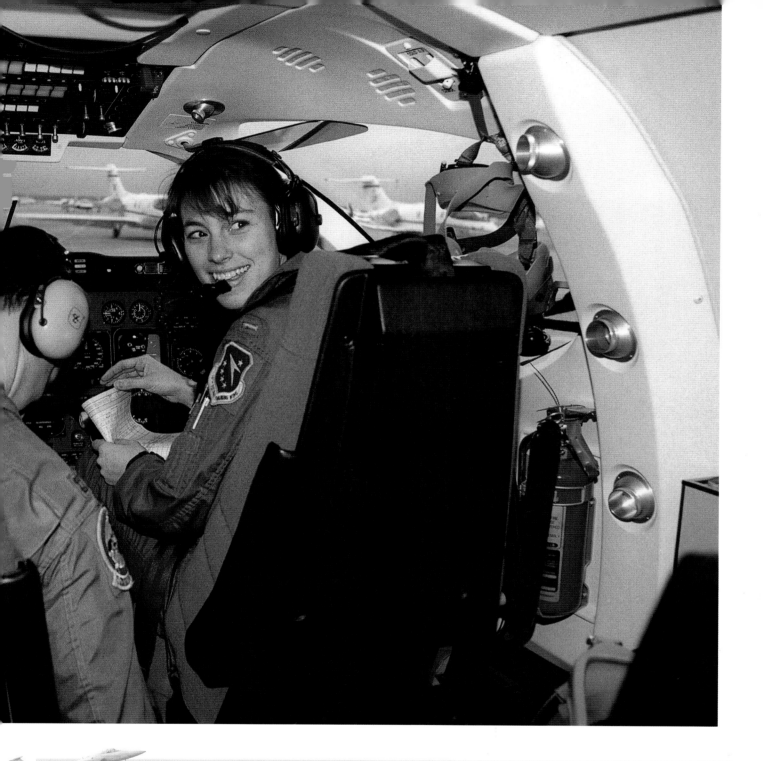

Laughlin Air Force Base is the largest pilot training facility in the world, and the third busiest airfield in the United States. It is not uncommon to see the skies around the runways filled with T-6As, T-37s, and T-38s, all jockeying in a precise dance for a landing order or a take off. More than 300 flights a day leave Laughlin. There is more radio traffic there than on most bases, and students must have situational awareness, which is good practice for real-world flying. Students train at Laughlin 365 days a year, and more than 12,000 students have passed thorough its doors.

A pilot and crew chief go over maintenance records before a flight in a T-38C Talon.

Instructors take T-1A students through every possible mission, including low-level tactics, 500 feet off the deck, long-distance planning and navigation, and air refueling techniques, with two feet of tail-to-belly separation.

Finally, after hours of preparation it is time to fly. The T-1A's handling characteristics and technology are much different from those of the Tweet or Texan II training aircraft. Students are introduced to the autopilot and glass cockpit, a series of television-like screens that display some of the flight instruments. The T-37 preflight planning, like the mission itself, typically lasts a few hours. A T-1A flight may involve a two-hour brief, followed by a three- or four-hour flight, followed by a two-hour postflight debrief. Learning new aircraft systems and absorbing new information, all while trying to keep up with growing mountains of paperwork, is challenging. Students begin to feel that this is the most difficult task they have ever set out to accomplish in their lives.

CST provided Captain Scott O'Grady with the knowledge he needed to stay alive and evade capture after his F-16 was shot down over Bosnia in 1996. O'Grady had three goals: survive, evade the enemy, and make radio contact with friendly forces. He had some food, water, a radio, and a global positioning system (GPS). By the sixth day, he was cold, hungry, and exhausted, but he would not give up. He had successfully evaded the enemy, but had run out of food and water and survived on grass and ants. One night while it was raining, O'Grady just faced the sky and opened his mouth to drink the raindrops. He even managed to collect about a pint of rainwater in a plastic bag for later use. The Air Force had heard his radio calls and sent in a special United States Marine Corps 42-member tactical recovery aircraft and personnel (TRAP) force, a team that rescues downed pilots behind enemy lines. O'Grady made it home, in large part because of his survival training.

A pair of F-16s flying in a two-ship formation, similar to the formation Captain Scott O'Grady was flying when he was shot down.

Working long hours, students are challenged daily by various forms of adversity. It is tough, but those who really want to be there and earn their silver wings will somehow survive each day.

Unlike the days in the Tweet, where airsickness was a concern, the T-1A flies like a private Learjet. But it still takes some getting used to. The new, larger airplane is faster and more maneuverable than the Tweet.

Students' routines are now changing dramatically. The EPs are reduced to one a week instead of every day. Pilots will work with their copilots on CRM, formation flying, navigation, and more. The T-1A phase culminates with the nav checkride. This takes three to four hours of flying and about the same amount of time in the brief and debrief.

The last portion of T-1A school involves three formation flights, three formation airdrop flights, and four air-refueling flights, in preparation for missions in the KC-135. Then comes the final checkride.

TURBOPROP TRACK

Some students elect the twin turboprop T-44 (the Air Force C-12) training at Naval Air Station, Corpus Christi, Texas. Those students will go on to fly the turboprop C-130 Hercules. The training profiles closely resemble typical missions flown by the C-130. As with the other tracks, students live a life of flying and studying, with some sleep, six days a week. But the routine does vary. One day students show up at 0400, and the next day they show up at noon for a night flight. It is difficult to get used

A pair of C-12s fly in formation. The twin turboprop T-44 (C-12) is used to train pilots going to the turboprop track.

AIR FORCE PILOT CODE OF CONDUCT:

Article I

I am an American fighting in the forces which guard my country and our way of life. I am prepared to give my life in their defense.

Article II

I will never surrender of my own free will. If in command, I will never surrender the members of my command while they still have the means to resist.

Article III

If I am captured, I will continue to resist by all means available. I will make every effort to escape and aid others to escape. I will accept neither parole nor special favors from the enemy.

Article IV

If I become a prisoner of war, I will keep faith with my fellow prisoners. I will give no information or take part in any action, which might be harmful to my comrades. If I am senior, I will take command. If not, I will obey the lawful orders of those appointed over me and will back them up in every way.

Article V

When questioned, should I become a prisoner of war, I am required to give name, rank, service number and date of birth. I will evade answering further questions to the utmost of my ability. I will make no oral or written statements disloyal to my country and its allies or harmful to their cause.

Article VI

I will never forget that I am an American, fighting for freedom, responsible for my actions, and dedicated to the principles which made my country free. I will trust in my God and in the United States of America.

to the schedule, and so much information must be absorbed that it's like drinking from a firehose all over again.

HELICOPTER TRACK

Other students selected to fly helicopters complete their training at the 23rd Flying Training Squadron (23 FTS) at Air Force specialized undergraduate pilot training helicopter (SUPT-H) at Fort Rucker, Alabama. They train on the UH-1N Huey. The helicopter syllabus includes operational skills such as low-level flying and combat tactics training. Phase I, the initial rotary wing qualification course (RWQC), includes basic helicopter transition, maneuvers, emergency procedures, navigation, and instrument flight of about 46 flight hours, and 51 hours of flight simulator instruction. There are another nine hours of computer-based training (CBT) lessons.

Phase I and Phase II together require approximately 23 to 26 weeks to complete and cover 145 hours of hands-on training per student, with 112 hours of actual helicopter flying, and includes instrument procedures,

remote operating procedures, low-level flight, navigation, approach, departure, basic formation flight, and night procedures. Students learn to employ aircraft weapons, fly in formation while aerial refueling, or land on U.S. Navy ships underway at night. No other aircraft in the Air Force inventory flies such an array of missions.

Academics usually start around 0700 and last anywhere from one to three hours. Students arrive for the 1045 brief, which covers safety issues, daily questions, and any unusual flight operations. Then each student receives their specific mission brief from their instructors.

At 1200, the students pick up life-support gear and aircraft keys. The standard sortie is three hours long, with each student flying for half of the flight. Most sorties involve a takeoff from Lowe Army Heliport, and a flight to Stinson or Shelly stage field. Flying at the stage field involves such maneuvers as pattern work, slopes, hovering, and auto-rotations, followed by a return to Lowe Army Heliport. By 1600, the daily sortie and debrief are complete, and students are released from the flightline on an individual basis.

Kenyan workers unload bags of flour from U.S. Air Force cargo pallets. Each worker carried a 110-pound bag of flour to a waiting truck. The C-141 Starlifter in the background carried seven pallets with more than 450 bags and 50,000 pounds of flour to Wajir. The aircraft belonged to the 63rd Airlift Wing, Norton Air Force Base, California, and was flown by an aircrew from the 14th Airlift Squadron, Charleston Air Force Base, South Carolina.

Air Force Special Operations, along with other groups, was part of the team that captured and transported Manuel Noriega, president of Panama and drug lord, to the United States for trial.

By now, countless hours have been spent in the cockpit, in simulators, and in the classroom. It has been a full year of exhaustive flight training, but now all of this hard work finally culminates in graduation.

GRADUATION

After successfully completing JSUPT, officers receive their silver wings and are awarded the aeronautical rating of pilot. Young pilots play an important role in America's future. Some will go into combat, others will fly relief supplies and food to victims of disaster and famine.

"They'll make a big difference, not just for the United States, but for all the people in the world that they'll help," said one Colonel. "And when they leave training, they understand that."

These new pilots are now ready to fly for the Air Force, but they will still need more training. Most will report to their next base and start training in their assigned aircraft.

The C-9 ambulance aircraft over the St. Louis arch.

Captain Connie Engle was the first woman in the Air Force to solo.

The successful completion of pilot training during World War II was not without a heavy price. From January 1941 to August 1945, 191,654 cadets were awarded pilot wings. However, 132,993 "washed out" or were killed during training, a loss rate of approximately 69 percent.

Once prohibited by the Combat Exclusion Law from flying in combat, women now fly fighters and bombers into harm's way, and female Air Force pilots are becoming more common.

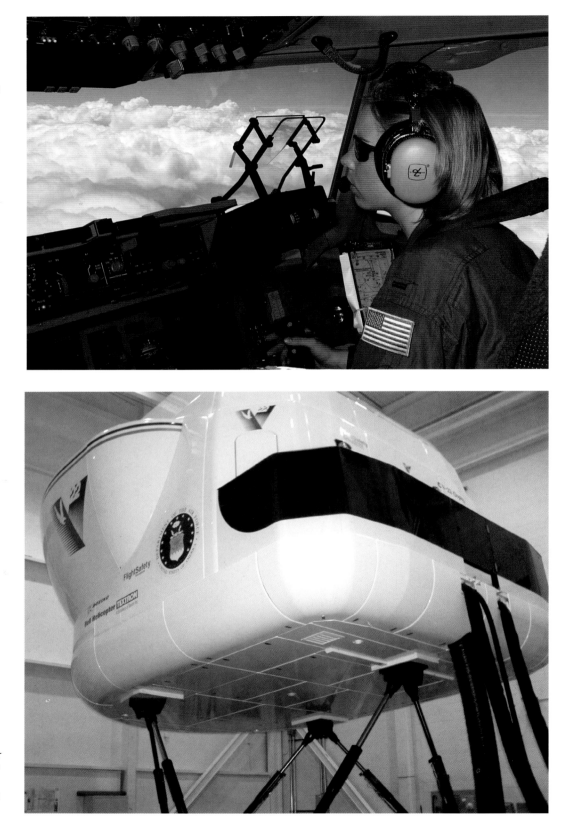

The F-22 Raptor simulator is a full-motion simulator that provides test pilots with their first experience in the newest fighter.

Captain Jennifer Wilson, a B-2 Spirit pilot, was the first female B-2 pilot to fly a combat mission. The B-2 has a crew of two pilots: an aircraft commander and a mission commander. The B-2 is intended to deliver gravity nuclear bombs or 40,000 pounds of conventional weapons, including precision-guided standoff weapons, joint direct-attack munitions (JDAM), and joint air-to-surface standoff missiles. It is equipped with a color, nine-tube, electronic flight instrumentation system (EFIS), which displays flight, engine, and sensor data, as well as information on avionics systems and weapons status. The pilot can choose to activate the appropriate selection of flight and mission equipment for take-off mode, go-to-war mode, and landing mode by using a simple three-way switch. The aircraft carries all its weapons internally and is fitted with two separate weapons bays in the center of the aircraft.

An Air Force IP, left, prepares his student, a naval officer, for an exchange-program training sortie. The JSUPT program provides Navy and Marine pilots, navigators, and engineers an opportunity to fly in various Air Force aircraft.

Fighting Falcons from the 21st Fighter Squadron refuel from a KC-10 Extender over southern Arizona. The KC-10 has light strips called "captain's bars," a green, yellow, and red strip on the wings. The pilot of the aircraft taking on fuel drives to the green strip, while the "boomer" in the tanker "flies" the boom into a one-foot hole containing the refueling receptacle in the jet. The KC-10 is the military version of the DC-10 commercial airliner.

The F-15 is one of the world's best fighter platforms and the first choice of many student pilots.

No longer in its World War II war paint, this BT-19 was an Army Air Force trainer named the Vultee Valiant, but dubbed by its pilots the "Vultee Vibrator." *Henry M. Holden*

The Academy's first class of female pilots, who graduated in 1977, included (left to right) Captains Susan Rogers, Mary Donahue, and Christine Schott; First Lieutenant Victoria Crawford; Captains Connie Engle and Kathy La Sauce; First Lieutenants Carol Scherer and Sandra Scott; and Second Lieutenants Mary Livingston and Kathleen Rambo.

The Army Air Force used WACO CG-4 gliders in several assaults in Europe during World War II. Glider pilots and their silent wings were born in the combat of that war, and they faded from the scene when the war ended. Gliders gave commanders an innovative way to move troops and equipment into battle behind enemy lines. However, this tactic required specialized training for pilots. The first students—many of whom had been eliminated from other types of flight training or were considered too old for regular flight training—received up to eight weeks of ground and air training with an emphasis on landing techniques in the standard 48-foot-long CG-4A glider. The gliders had only the most basic flight instruments: turn and bank indicator, air speed, vertical speed, and compass. Training included an advanced phase requiring 40 landings under full-load conditions and instruction in after-landing procedures. Approximately 5,000 men became glider pilots. *Henry M. Holden collection*

The most widely used transport of World War II was the C-47. *National Archives*

FOUR

Mission Qualification

The Air Force has approximately 44 types of operational aircraft. After JSUPT, pilots move to follow-on training in a specialty before receiving an operational assignment. Assignments vary from flying the Air Force's premier fighter, the F-15E Strike Eagle, to their largest aircraft, the four-engine jet C-5A/B Galaxy transport. Assignments also include flying the B-1B Lancer bomber, the E-3 airborne early warning and control (AWACS), and various helicopters.

TRAINING BASES

The 19th Air Force of the AETC provides follow-on training for most regular duty Air Force, Air Force Reserve, and Air National Guard pilots. They have an inventory of 22 different types of rotary and fixed-wing aircraft.

The 97th Air Mobility Wing at Altus Air Force Base, Oklahoma, is the home of the Air Force's only strategic airlift, aerial delivery, and aerial refueling school. It provides training for pilots assigned to C-5 Galaxy, KC-135 Stratotanker, KC-10 Extender, and C-17 Globemaster III aircraft.

A close-up of a U.S. Air Force weapon systems officer in the cockpit of an F-16DJ Fighting Falcon during an air combat training mission.

Two KC-135 Stratotanker pilots conduct a preflight check. The cockpit is cramped, so pilots must instinctively know the purpose and location of every switch.

Aircrews assigned to fly the C-130 Hercules train at Little Rock Air Force Base, Arkansas. Pilots assigned to fly the MC-130H Combat Talon, HC-130P Combat Shadow aircraft, MH-53J Pave Low, or MH-60 Pave Hawk helicopters receive their training at the 58th Special Operations Wing, at Kirtland Air Force Base, New Mexico.

The 81st Training Wing at Keesler Air Force Base, Mississippi, provides training for pilots assigned to the C-21. At Fort Rucker, Alabama, the Army provides training in the C-12 Super King Air. Davis Monthan Air Force Base, Arizona, provides training in the A-10 Warthog. The 12th Flying Training Wing at Randolph Air Force Base, Texas, known for years as the "West Point of the Air," provides instructor pilots for the JSUPT bases. Sheppard Air Force Base also conducts its own pilot instructor training (PIT). Sheppard is a Euro NATO joint jet pilot training (ENJJPT) base. Instructors that train at Sheppard can only be assigned to Sheppard, though, since they operate on a different syllabus than the other JSUPT bases.

An Air Force HH-60 Pave Hawk has special radar that enables the crew to follow terrain contours and avoid obstacles. During Operation Anaconda in Afghanistan, two HH-60 Pave Hawk helicopters assigned to the 66th Expeditionary Rescue Squadron brought back critically wounded troops from a small valley surrounded on three sides by enemy forces. Entering the valley under intense small-arms fire, the first helicopter crew was targeted by machine guns, mortars, and rocket-propelled grenades. One mortar round detonated within 50 feet of the aircraft. As pararescuemen from the first aircraft began loading the injured, the flight crew guided the second aircraft to a safe landing while an AC-130 gunship provided close-air support. That night, the two crews rescued nine soldiers from the battlefield. The Pave Hawk aircrews all earned Distinguished Flying Crosses, one of the military's highest combat decorations.

The Pave Hawk is one of the largest helicopters in the Air Force fleet. It is 64 feet long and has a 54-foot main rotor with four rotor blades. The blades are made of fiberglass with edges of titanium and are filled with nitrogen gas, which makes them very light and strong.

An F-15E takes off using afterburners. The F-15E is the "tip of the spear" and can carry every fighter weapon in the Air Force inventory. This aircraft is from the 48th Fighter Wing stationed at Royal Air Force Base Lakenheath, United Kingdom.

COMBAT SURVIVAL TRAINING

Early in the mission qualification process, everyone visits Fairchild Air Force Base in Spokane, Washington, for the infamous combat survival training (CST). CST is also called survival, evasion, resistance, and escape (SERE) training. The first week is the academic and laboratory phase, in which students learn the skills needed to survive in enemy territory, in the wilderness, and in a variety of climates and conditions—ranging from desert to arctic.

Throughout the week, trainees learn all the steps from ejection to being rescued. They learn how to maintain survival gear, how to use maps and a compass for ground navigation, and camouflage techniques. They also spend a day in parachute training.

The week's schedule is crowded, with practically no downtime during the waking hours. Classes last all day, with trainees learning how to construct shelters using ponchos and parachute cord, learning how to sew signals made from orange parachute pieces, and figuring out evasion plans through a simulation of an airplane crash and ejection into enemy territory.

At the end of the first week, the trainees are bused about 60 miles north of Fairchild for six days of field training, where they learn how to hike through 4 to 6 feet of snow in snowshoes while carrying 60-pound packs.

An F-16 drops live ordnance during a training flight. This Fighting Falcon is from the Eighth Fighter Wing stationed at Kusan Air Base, Republic of Korea. With a LANTIRN targeting pod, the pilot can "see" through light smoke and haze and pick up hot spots on the battlefield. The pod also provides highly accurate information to help direct other fighters to targets or to self-designate and attack targets using an arsenal of GPS and laser-guided weapons available to the F-16.

A pilot lights a campfire as he takes part in survival training.

They learn fire-building techniques, plotting coordinates on a map, and navigating to a specific destination. Students learn how to create and use traps to catch small animals for food, what plants are edible, ways to acquire water, and methods of preparing food. They learn how to vector a rescue helicopter to their position using a radio and compass, and how to use smoke, flares, and signal mirrors.

The real test comes when the students are told to hike several miles into the woods, build a shelter, find food, build a fire, melt snow for water, and survive. Each pair of trainees is given coordinates that they must navigate to and a designated rendezvous time when they are to contact search-and-rescue (SAR) forces for further instructions. As they hike through the woods, "enemy troops" are looking for the "downed pilots." Eventually, the trainees are either "caught" by the "enemy," or they

A pilot attempts to contact rescue personnel during survival training.

A pilot sets off a smoke marker to attract attention as he takes part in survival training.

reach their destination, where a helicopter picks them up and returns them to camp.

Pilots who have completed ground-survival training at Fairchild will attend one week of water-survival training in Pensacola, Florida. Some aviators also go through arctic survival training at Eielson Air Force Base, Alaska. These three schools teach the skills required to survive in nearly any environment.

FUGE QUALIFICATION

The fast-moving fighter aircraft in today's Air Force are capable of producing extremely high G-loading on a pilot, even more than many physically-fit fighter pilots can withstand. Before the Air Force spends several million dollars training a fighter pilot, it must determine which individuals can withstand the sudden boost from 4 to 8 Gs that typically occurs during high-speed maneuvers. A prior trip to the centrifuge familiarized potential fighter pilots with the G-suit and gave them an opportunity to practice the anti-G-strain maneuver (AGSM). This trip to the fuge is different—the stakes are much higher. In order to qualify to fly their assigned fighter aircraft, they now must sustain a required G-force for a specified duration of time spinning in the fuge. A student's performance here will make or break their chances to fly the fast movers. This qualification spin happens after graduation from JSUPT and before introduction to fighter fundamentals (IFF).

With three American flags on board his fighter, this pilot prepares for a combat mission. "I have two in the front of the canopy to represent my two kids, and I carry one on me for my wife," he said.

When the potential fighter pilot has demonstrated to the rest of the class and to the IP that they are able to perform AGSM satisfactorily, they take five spins in the fuge. The first spin is without a G-suit and is designed to find the student's G tolerance, or resting level without AGSM (usually between 3.5 and 4.5 Gs). It begins at 1.5 Gs and builds in increments of 0.1 G until the fuge reaches 8 Gs. At a point where the student begins to experience light loss and tunnel vision, they begin the AGSM. As the G forces are increased, the student feels like they are being crushed and suffocated by an invisible force of one-half ton. The student may experience gray-out, and little red dots may appear under the skin, indicating that capillaries have broken. The student can terminate the spin at any time by releasing the control stick.

This is a non-retribution spin that allows the student to find out where their resting G tolerance is without penalty. If the student releases the stick on this spin, they are simply keeping themselves from G-LOCing. Later, if they release the control stick, it is a de facto removal from fast-mover training.

The second spin is with a G-suit and increases the student's use of AGSM. It begins quickly, with the initial level set 1 G above the resting level for 30 seconds. During this period, the student tenses their muscles and focuses on their breathing.

The third spin is the qualifying spin; if the student is going to fly a fighter, they have to endure up to 9 Gs for 15 seconds. By now, the student is physically exhausted and still has two spins to go.

This pilot inspects the left-side-mounted AIM 9 L/M sidewinder heat-seeking missile.

This is the small but uncluttered cockpit of an F-16 fighter. Note the canted seat. *Henry M. Holden*

An F-16CJ Fighting Falcon bristles with ordnance. It can carry one M-61A1 20mm multibarrel canncn with 500 rounds; external stations can carry up to six air-to-air missiles, conventional air-to-air and air-to-surface munitions, and electron c countermeasure pods. The "SW" tail code indicates it is from the 20th Fighter Wing at Shaw Air Force Base, South Carolina.

Above: An F-15E
Strike Eagle from
the 494th Fighter
Squadron of the 48th
Fighter Wing takes to
the skies en route
to a deployment
supporting Operation
Iraqi Freedom.

An A-10, F-15E, F-15C,
and F-16D fly over
Lake Mead in a
fingertip formation.

Each fighter has a specific qualification spin: F-15E, upright seat, 7.5 Gs for 15 seconds; F-15C, upright seat, 9 Gs for 15 seconds; F-16, canted seat (angled back 35 degrees), 8 Gs for 15 seconds; and A-10, upright seat, 7.5 Gs for 15 seconds.

If the student has made it this far, the next spin is the easiest. The "check six" spin lasts for 10 seconds, while the student looks over their shoulder at their six o'clock position.

The last spin is the air combat maneuver (ACM), which simulates a dogfight. The HUD shows the tail view of a computer-generated enemy jet fighter with a horizon and landscape. The student pulls the stick back, puts the enemy airplane in the HUD crosshairs, and shoots. The spin lasts for about a minute, with four "gunfights," all in the 7- to 8-G range. The first one is a challenge, but physically it is a rapid downhill ride. By the last gunfight, the student is out of muscle energy, and on the verge of G-LOC. Those who make it through the test will learn to fly the most sophisticated fighter weapons platforms in the world.

Brigadier General Leon Johnson, chairman of the Air Force Reserve Command Human Resources Development Council, presents a gift to retired Air Force Colonel Charles McGee, president of Tuskegee Airmen International. McGee is one of the original Tuskegee Airmen, a group of African-Americans who, at a time of racial segregation in the military, answered the call to arms and trained at Tuskegee, Alabama. They later flew fighters on ground-attack and bomber-escort missions over North Africa and Europe during World War II. They earned more than 150 awards and medals and during escort missions never lost a bomber to enemy fighters.

After the fuge, fighter pilot students attend Introduction to Fighter Fundamentals (IFF), a six-week course in the AT-38, before reporting to their aircraft training school.

INTRODUCTION TO FIGHTER FUNDAMENTALS

All pilots assigned to fighter aircraft complete the IFF course at either Moody Air Force Base, flying the new, glass-cockpit T-38C, or Sheppard Air Force Base, Texas, flying the AT-38B. The IFF curriculum is designed to teach basic fighter maneuvers and tactics to new pilots or weapons systems officers (WSO), the "backseater" in the F-15E.

The length of IFF training is from two to three months. At IFF, the trainee goes through the A track (all air-to-air) if they are going to the F-15C, the B track for F-16s and F-15Es (an even portion of air-to-air and air-to-ground), and the C track for A-10s (some air-to-air, mostly air-to-ground). All three tracks take the same amount of time for the average trainee.

FIGHTER TRAINING UNIT

Upon completion of IFF, pilots go to a fighter training unit (FTU), where they will spend up to nine months learning various weapons systems associated with their weapons platform. Washouts at this point are few and are usually due to a lack of situational awareness and an inability to grasp fighter discipline. During this post-graduate course, pilots learn advanced tactical formation flying, low-level navigation, air-to-ground weapons delivery, and offensive, defensive, and high-aspect fighter maneuvers.

Each pilot completes a designated track of study, depending on the follow-on aircraft (the aircraft to which the pilot will eventually be assigned). Each track consists of about 19 sorties tailored to meet the requirements of a particular airframe.

A pilot signals his crew chief for a number-two engine start.

Situational awareness—as demonstrated here with a C-130 pilot—is essential to aircrew safety. A pilot must constantly scan the sky around and behind him for other traffic.

Some pilots move on to train in the F-15 Eagle at Tyndall Air Force Base, Florida, which is also the home of the first F-22 Raptor training squadron. F-15E Strike Eagle pilots train at Seymour-Johnson Air Force Base, North Carolina.

F-16 Fighting Falcon pilots train at Luke Air Force Base, Arizona. Luke Air Force Base is the only active Air Force base where initial pilot training (IPT) is taught on the F-16. Some trainees (active, Guard, or Reserve) may go to Tucson International Airport to train with the Reserve unit there. Others may go to Kelly Field, San Antonio, to train at the Air National Guard FTU. This course consists of 80 hours of training, and takes the pilot from their first introduction to the F-16 through basic-mission qualification to join an operational squadron as a wingman. Pilots practice training missions over the huge, 2.7-million-acre Barry M. Goldwater Range in the Sonoran Desert.

Even in this fast-paced, intense training environment, 98 percent of students graduate. Most attrition tends to occur during JSUPT, although a few may be unable to handle the often overwhelming demands and pace of the curriculum.

The pilot training is identical for reservists, Air National Guard, and regular-duty Air Force pilots. A normal day starts with a pre-dawn mission brief, followed by a one-hour flight, with an even longer debrief. Afterward, the instructors grade the trainees on every aspect of the mission. Once the entire process is complete, the schedule is repeated in the afternoon, either with the same trainee and mission profile, or a new trainee and an entirely different mission profile.

MISSION QUALIFICATION TRAINING

Following the completion of FTU, to become combat qualified in a specific airframe, the pilot moves to their squadron and mission qualification training (MQT), which lasts about three months. This is the first active flying assignment for a new pilot in which they will become fully mission qualified on real-world missions.

For the first few sorties, the pilot flies with an IP on their wing. The IP grades their performance and suggests areas that need attention. During this period, they learn dogfighting, bomb drops, and ground-threat avoidance. From the time the student leaves JSUPT to the time they achieve fully combat qualified status in the F-15E, for example, it takes about two-and-one-half to three years.

Right: Time-lapse photos show an F-16 launching a missile.

Below: An Air National Guard pilot with the 184th Bomb Wing, 127th Bomb Squadron, McConnell Air Force Base, Kansas, flies a training mission in the flight/mission simulator for the B-1B Lancer aircraft.

Once fully qualified, the pilot flies the number-two slot (wing position) in a two-ship formation for about one-and-one-half to two years. They then move on to 2-FLUG (two-ship flight lead upgrade), in which they take about 10 upgrade rides as a flight lead trainee. They then take the lead in a two-ship formation. If they progress satisfactorily, they move up to four-ship flight lead upgrade (4-FLUG) of a four-ship formation, about four to six months after completion of 2-FLUG.

After upgrading to four-ship flight lead and showing keen abilities in leading a four-ship formation, the pilot may be selected for instructor pilot upgrade (IPLUG) training. Instructional and supervisory experience is an important step in a pilot's career path to becoming a senior officer. Pilots interested in becoming future commanders should gain instructional experience by serving in a combat crew training squadron (CCTS).

On August 20, 1910, the first shot was fired from an airplane, at Sheepshead Bay racetrack in Brooklyn, New York. With Glenn Curtiss piloting, Lieutenant Jacob E. Fickel fired a rifle at a 3x5-foot target from an altitude of 100 feet.

When a pilot is first assigned to a major weapon system (MWS), they gain technical experience in aircraft systems, crew management if appropriate, and the unit's various missions for an average of four years before upgrading to instructor pilot. An MWS is any non-training aircraft to which a new pilot is assigned following JSUPT. It does not necessarily have actual weapons. For example, an E-3C AWACS is considered an MWS, but it neither carries nor employs weapons of any kind. After upgrading to IP in their MWS, the pilot may be selected as a flight evaluator (FE), whose primary responsibility is giving periodic mission qualification and instrument checkrides to the other members of their squadron.

Training never really ends. As long as an aviator wears the silver wings of an Air Force pilot, they receive continual training, so they are ready—at a moment's notice—to defend America.

WEAPONS INSTRUCTOR COURSE

After completing MQT, and only after upgrading to IP in their MWS, about 10 percent of pilots will qualify for the weapons instructor course (WIC). Weapons school provides Air Force

This E-3 AWACS Sentry in flight is based at the 552nd Air Control Wing at Tinker Air Force Base, Oklahoma.

graduate-level training for instructors for the A-10, B-1, B-2, B-52, EC-130, F-15, F-15E, F-16, HH-60, RC-135, command and control operations, intelligence, and space weapons. In WIC, the pilot studies every operational aspect of their MWS.

Selection to attend the weapons school is highly competitive. Of those who qualify, less than five percent are actually selected to attend. Students begin the course in a rigorous core academic program that features intense classroom study and hands-on training with actual equipment. This training prepares students to get the most out of the flying and mission phases. The culmination of this five-and-one-half month program is the mission-employment phase. During this phase, the courses are combined into a large, mixed-force exercise. Students are exposed to the entire range of air and space combat capabilities and are required to plan the exercise and integrate the different weapons systems and disciplines to effectively accomplish the objectives of each simulated wartime scenario.

Graduates return to their units as weapons officers, serving as their wing's technical expert in weapons, weapon systems, force integration, employment tactics, and training procedures and techniques. As the commander's technical advisor, the weapons officer is the focal point for the design and execution of appropriate training programs that will improve the unit's wartime capability. To equate Air Force pilot training to civilian education, JSUPT would be considered the baccalaureate level, FTU/MQT would be master's level, and WIC would be doctorate level.

Even after earning pilot wings, there is a never-ending process to maintain currency and qualification in various stages of flying—from instrument approaches, landings, air refueling, etc. "I was on a night refueling mission, on the wing of a KC-135," said an F-15E Strike Eagle pilot. "There was no moon, and very little ambient light. I slowly noticed the nav lights on the tanker were appearing in a different orientation than I expected." (The KC-135 has nacelle lights and wing-tip lights, but no strip lights, as does the KC-10.) "I suddenly realized that I was nearly inverted over the tanker, and very close—too close. I recovered, pulled away, and let my wingman tank up. After that, I had a much greater appreciation for how quickly the human mind can play tricks on you and allow you to get into dangerous situations."

With initial training complete, pilots accumulate flight hours, and continue to study the aircraft's systems and upgrades. Fighter pilots have to know every piece of equipment on their aircraft, plus understand the nature of intelligence threats, and for this they may require a higher security clearance. F-15E Strike Eagle pilots require a top-secret SCI (sensitive compartmented information) clearance.

WOMEN FIGHTER PILOTS

What had been an exclusive brotherhood until 1993 is becoming a brother- and-sisterhood of the United States

An F-15 approaches a refueling boom.

Colonel Charles DeBellevue was the first Air Force weapons systems officer to become an ace during the Vietnam War, in 1972. DeBellevue scored his first four aerial victories while crewing with Captain Steve Ritchie, who became the first Air Force ace of the war. DeBellevue became the second, and America's top "MiG Killer," when he downed two more on September 9, 1972, while on a four-ship combat air patrol with Captain John Madden, his F-4 Phantom pilot. The six MiG total was the most earned during the war.

Out of more than 12,000 Air Force pilots, about 460 are women. There are 46 female fighter pilots in the Air Force, according to the Air Force Personnel Center, Randolph Air Force Base, Texas.

Air Force's best and bravest. When the combat exclusion law was repealed in 1993 because of the performance of women pilots in the 1991 Persian Gulf War, women pilots in the Air Force finally had access to combat training in fighters.

Male or female, fighter pilot training is not for the faint of heart. "The training is tough," said one pilot. "If you're ultra-sensitive, you're in the wrong profession."

To succeed as fighter pilots, women have to be able to dish out what the men dish out. They need a fighter pilot mentality. "This job is not harder for women; it is just different," said one female F-16 pilot. "We get up everyday, put on our flight suits, and walk proudly into our fighter squadron knowing how blessed we are to have the opportunity to serve our country, and a cause greater than ourselves."

"Women fighter pilots are tough," another female pilot said. "You have to be willing to kill people, and be ready to die."

If there were problems fitting into this "brotherhood," another woman pilot found the solution: "I learned at the Academy that the only way to fit in is to be yourself. Women who choose to fly fighters are much like the men who choose to fly fighters. As soon

Jeannie Flynn became the first F-15 female pilot after the revocation of the Combat Exclusion Law.

As seen from the aircraft's rear seat, the pilot of an F-15D aircraft banks to the right to follow another aircraft during a training flight.

as male pilots see that female pilots are just as capable as they are, most of the problems go away." And all fighter pilots—male and female—hone their skills at Red Flag.

RED FLAG

Red Flag is a fighter pilot training program administered through the 414th Combat Training Squadron, at Nellis Air Force Base. The squadron has been Red Flag combat

training for almost 30 years. Their goal: increase aircrew survival by simulating the first 10 combat missions a pilot would fly in a war.

Red Flag was created because of the staggering losses of Air Force aircrews in the Vietnam War. In the Korean War, aircrews maintained a ten-to-one kill ratio. During Vietnam, the kill ratio dropped to about three to one. This led Air Force officials to search for a solution. They concluded that the Air Force's lack of dissimilar air-to-air

air forces can train. Inside this battlefield, aircrews train to fight together, survive together, and win together. These pilots and flying units are not in competition against one another.

In a typical Red Flag exercise, Blue Air (friendly) engages Red Air (hostile) in combat situations. Blue Air is made up of units from ACC, AMC, U.S. Air Force Europe, Pacific air forces (PACAF), ANG, USAFR, Army, Navy, Marine, and allied air forces. Red Air is composed of Red Flag's Adversary Tactics Division flying the F-16, and provides air threats through the emulation of enemy tactics. Other U.S. Air Force, Navy, and Marine units flying in concert with electronic ground defenses and communications and radar jamming equipment often augment Red Air.

All fighter pilots participate in a Red Flag competition several times in their flying careers. No one is "chosen" to go because of superior skill, as the training is valuable for every pilot in the squadron.

"Red Flag saves lives," said one commander of the 414th Combat Training Squadron. "We can push the envelope here without getting anyone hurt. This is the most intense environment in the world today, other than when people are shooting for real."

During the Persian Gulf War, an F-16 pilot had just returned from a mission over Baghdad. Anti-aircraft rounds and surface-to-air missiles had plagued his mission, not to mention his aircraft. After landing, he encountered a news crew asking about the intensity of his flight. The F-16 pilot turned to the reporter and said, "This is really tough, but it's not as intense as my Red Flag missions were."

Red Air's charter is to educate Blue Air. Make Blue Air pilots better, and ensure they learn. "We can replicate any air threat," the commander said. "We're the only unit in the Air Force—maybe the world—that can do that."

Red Flag is a place where pilots like one with the call sign "Preacher Bob" hone their skills, and at times, have some fun. "During a night Red Flag training flight," recalls Preacher Bob, "the moon was out, and we were down to low altitude on night-vision goggles, running at about 500 miles per hour. The Nellis airspace is full of mountains, so to evade the threats from both air and ground that were looking for us, we stayed as close to the ground as we could. This meant popping over the top of ridgelines then pulling near-inverted over the other side. In the daytime, this type of maneuvering is standard. At night, though, it was a pure adrenaline rush. The end

combat training (DACT) and knowledge about Soviet tactics and capabilities were major contributors to the degradation of U.S. pilot air-to-air combat skills. Red Flag was the answer.

Red Flag pilots come from flying units around the Air Force. Sometimes the Navy, Marines, Army, and allied forces take part too. Every Red Flag exercise is comprised of one to three periods, each of which is two weeks long.

Since combat is no place to train aircrews, Red Flag provides a peacetime "battlefield" within which our combat results were bombs 'on target' and all aircraft returning alive and undamaged. In the type of Red Flag scenario and threat array we were flying against, that's quite an accomplishment. With that training, all of us knew that if we had to do that very same thing in actual combat, we absolutely could."

HERCULES IN HARM'S WAY

The C-130 Hercules (Herc) is more than 50 years old and is the oldest operational aircraft in the Air Force. It picked up its nickname "Hercules" from its ability to haul heavy loads. Herc pilots do not have the glamour associated with fighter pilots, but Herc pilots put it on the line as often.

The 109th Airlift Wing of the New York National Guard is the only Hercules unit in the world that flies the ski-equipped LC-130. The 109th's missions range from Greenland to McMurdo Station, on the edge of Antarctica. While many tactical C-130 aircrews often fly at night, in blackout conditions, the 109th operates only in daylight, but often in whiteout conditions that mimic flying inside a ping-pong ball. Aircrews flying LC-130

The AC-130U Spectre is a variation on the basic C-130 Hercules. The Spectre gunship is armed with 25mm and 40mm cannons and a 105mm gun. It is used against enemy troops on the ground.

A U.S. Air Force C-130E Hercules flies over the Cape Hatteras Lighthouse on the North Carolina coast. The Hercules, capable of operating from rough dirt landing strips, is the Air Force's prime transport for intra-theater airlifts, dropping paratroops and equipment into hostile or remote areas.

Above: It is common for the LC-130 to use several miles of skiway to take off.

Left: The four turboprop engines on the C-130E/H/J give it a speed of 345 to 417 miles per hour at 20,000 feet. The aircraft is 97 feet, 9 inches long; 38 feet, 3 inches tall; and has a wingspan of 132 feet, 7 inches. It has a ceiling of 33,000 feet with a 45,000-pound payload.

missions must rely on special training to successfully complete a mission. For example, takeoff runs for a standard C-130 are usually several thousand feet. An LC-130 crew usually has takeoff "slides" of several miles before the aircraft gets airborne.

Basic aircrew qualification for the LC-130 begins at Little Rock Air Force Base, Arkansas, where they train for only single-ship airdrops in clear visibility. The pilots then go through C-130E and H-model training at Stratton Air National Guard Base, near Schenectady, New York. There they will fly with an IP in one of the 109th's wheeled C-130 aircraft. Pilots transition to fly the LC-130 either in Greenland or Antarctica. Pilots will fly with an IP for several weeks, practicing radar approaches and actual landings in weather. The final exam is a two-part hands-on test. The first part requires the copilot to fly to an ice-bound camp and land on the ice. The second part is taking off from the ice using assisted takeoff (ATO) rocket bottles to get airborne. It usually takes about twice as long for an LC-130 copilot to become fully qualified as it does for a copilot flying a standard C-130.

Crew resource management is essential to landing an LC-130 safely. The aircraft commander (AC) sets up for final approach about 10 miles out. The navigator briefs the crew on the skiway, weather, any obstacles or buildings, and where they are in relation to the flightpath. The navigator brings the ship down to about 300 feet AGL, about one mile out. Meanwhile, the copilot is watching for the skiway, and calling airspeed. In weather, the loadmaster lies on their stomach on the cockpit floor, peers thorough the lower windows, and helps look for a set of flags that marks the boundaries of the skiway. Once the flags are spotted, the copilot takes over from the navigator, and sets the flaps. At 50 feet, the flight engineer calls altitude in increments of 10 feet. The copilot calls the vertical speed and drift, while the AC lands the airplane.

What complicates the landing is that the AC is usually landing on instruments, and the proximity to the earth's magnetic poles sometimes confuses the instruments. The radar altimeter is less accurate on snow or ice, and the blowing snow often creates whiteout conditions.

Taking off is no less dangerous. The objective seems simple: crank up the aircraft to 65 knots, and lift the nose. At that point the aircraft will fly. However, the extreme cold (-40 degrees Fahrenheit), parasitic drag from the skis, weight of the cargo, and the winds make five- to eight-mile takeoff rolls common, and sometimes the LC-130 must go as far as 20 miles to get airborne. The eight ATO rocket bottles help, but only if they are fired at precisely the right time. They provide the power of an additional engine for about 20 seconds, power needed to give the airplane the boost it needs to lift the nose. Once the nose lifts, the wings will take the Herc into the sky.

The F-117A Nighthawk has flat panels placed at angles to scatter radar energy away from the airplane and into space, not back to the enemy radar set. In spite of hundreds of Iraqi anti-aircraft sites and Russian-built surface-to-air missiles (SAMs), not one of the 36 F-117s that flew 1,300 combat missions in Operation Desert Storm was shot down, or even scratched. The F-117A was invisible!

THE AIR FORCE GOES INVISIBLE

Until the 1991 Persian Gulf War, the F-117A Nighthawk, the Air Force's first stealth fighter, was untested in combat. Some wondered if the black jet was actually invisible to enemy radar. "I had mixed emotions the evening of January 16, 1991," said one F-117A pilot. "In the back of my mind I wondered, would this stealth really work? After all, we were flying into the heart of the Iraqi air defense system."

As the first wave of 10 F-117A fighters, code named "Thunder," rolled in over Baghdad, there was no anti-aircraft fire coming up. "It appeared that no one knew I was in the sky," said the pilot.

The pilot aimed the crosshairs of his weapons system on a bridge, and depressed a button on his throttle. The computer took over. "My laser began to flash as I tracked the target," said the pilot. "I pressed the 'pickle' button, felt the weapons bay doors snap open, and felt the 2,000-pound bomb drop from the aircraft. The doors slammed shut, and I watched on my infrared screen as the bomb went through the target. Stealth technology really worked."

OPERATION IRAQI FREEDOM

The skill and bravery of Air Force pilots are major reasons for Operation Iraqi Freedom's early successes. An A-10 Warthog, flown by an Air Force captain identified only by her call sign, "K.C.," was hit over Baghdad during a close-air-support mission. "We were very aware that it was a high-threat environment over Baghdad," she said. "At the same time, those are the risks you are going to take to help the guys on the ground. That's our job, that's what we do."

After K.C. delivered her ordnance, and was departing the target, "I felt the jet get hit. It was pretty obvious—it was loud," K.C. said.

After sustaining the hit, the aircraft immediately became uncontrollable. K.C. was over hostile territory, and the jet had lost all hydraulics. The jet rolled left and

A-10 Warthog.

Pilots of the A-10 Thunderbolt provide close-air support for ground forces. Affectionately called the "Warthog," the A-10 made a reputation with its tank-killing prowess during Operation Desert Storm. Because of its great flexibility, the A-10 can escort helicopters and C-130s, sanitize areas under air-refueling orbits, search for missile batteries, and conduct search and rescue and air interdiction. These two Warthogs are from the 104th Fighter Wing, Barnes MAP, Massachusetts.

pointed toward the ground. "It was an uncomfortable feeling being over Baghdad," she said. "The entire caution panel lit up, and the jet wasn't responding to any of my control inputs." This is where Air Force pilot training kicked in. K.C. had spent hundreds of hours in simulators and actual practice missions preparing for the worst-

case scenario, and suddenly, here she was, her aircraft damaged and spinning out of control.

An A-10 can survive direct hits from armor-piercing and high-explosive projectiles up to 23mm. K.C. knew this, but because the aircraft had sustained hits at the rear, including the horizontal stabilizer, tail section, and engine

cowling, K.C. could not see the damage. Her flight leader positioned his aircraft where he could see the damage. "The jet was flying pretty good, and the damage had not affected the flight control surfaces or the [landing] gear. If she could keep it flying, we would get out of Baghdad, and might be able to make it [back to base]," he said.

K.C. tried several different procedures to get the aircraft under control, but none worked. The Warthog has a triple-redundant hydraulic system. If primary hydraulics are shot away, the pilot switches to secondary. If secondary does not function, they must shift to manual reversion. This is like driving a Mack truck without power steering or power brakes. K.C. had to work the flight controls

KC surveys the battle damage to her A-10 Thunderbolt, which was hit over Baghdad during a close-air-support mission.

An F-117A is shown in flight. The initial attack that targeted Saddam Hussein in Operation Iraqi Freedom was led by two F-117 Nighthawks.

(rudder, elevator, ailerons, and flaps) without hydraulic assist. The aircraft began responding. "This was a good feeling because there is no way I wanted to eject over Baghdad," she said.

K.C. landed the Warthog safely, but stopping it and keeping it on the runway was another story. Without hydraulics, K.C. did not have speed brakes, wheel brakes, or steering. Alternating engine thrusts, she managed to keep the aircraft on the runway, and it stopped when it ran out of power.

Above: A B-1B Lancer drops cluster munitions. The CBU-105 is a GPS-guided precision cluster bomb which disburses bomblets that can home in on engine heat from an armored vehicle to deliver a fatal blow.

Right: Two F-15s from Barnes MAP, Massachusetts, are flying on a homeland security patrol.

Next page: An Air Force Pave Low is about to hook up with a C-130 for in-flight refueling.

Alone or in a group, the F-16 packs a powerful punch.

A C-17 pilot does a last check before taking off. The C-17 is capable of delivering a 66-ton Abrams tank to deployed army troops.

A view from inside a C-130 while it is refueling an HH-60 helicopter.

FIVE

Cross into the Blue

While Air Force pilots live exciting and sometimes dangerous lives, experience opens up new opportunities to them. They may be eligible for intensely challenging and sometimes secret assignments as reconnaissance pilots, test pilots, astronauts, or the newest pilot assignment, the RQ-1A/B Predator remotely piloted aircraft.

RECONNAISSANCE PILOTS

The U-2 program is a highly specialized weapons system that only highly experienced pilots may fly. Pilots come from a wide variety of aircraft backgrounds, including test pilots, fighter pilots, bomber pilots, tanker pilots, and instructor pilots. Requirements and skill levels are so extraordinarily high that only 38 percent of all applicants eventually become U-2 pilots. Experience weighs heavily in the selection process. Those selected for the interview phase must possess a strong flight evaluation history

This Thunderbird F-16C has a takeoff weight of 37,500 pounds. At its maximum performance, or "max performance takeoff," it can climb to 15,000 feet in about 25 seconds, giving the pilot an approximation of what astronauts feel while rocketing to outer space. With its afterburners ignited, it is assisted by more that 27,000 pounds of thrust as it clears the runway.

129

and the recommendation of their wing commander, in addition to far exceeding the 1,300 hours minimum flying time and meeting other requirements.

Requirements for applicants to the U-2 program include a minimum of 1,300 rated hours in crew aircraft (those having more than one pilot, including the T-1), or 800 rated hours as an instructor pilot in single-pilot aircraft (including the T-6, T-37, and T-38). This does not include student pilot time. The applicant must have a minimum of 18 months as an AC in primary mission aircraft (fighter, bomber, etc.). The pilot also needs a security clearance of top secret SBI/SCI (special background investigation, and sensitive compartmented information).

The entire U-2 community worldwide consists of 31 aircraft and fewer than 80 pilots, and offers unique challenges to those selected. The demanding high-altitude reconnaissance missions require motivated aviators with a high degree of self-confidence, professionalism, and an extraordinary combination of outstanding flying skill and common sense needed to conduct and survive dangerous missions. Operational sorties average five to nine hours at altitudes in excess of 85,000 feet, and require the use of a full pressure suit and helmet. Operational missions occur around the world, and the U-2 pilot must be prepared for a large variety of tactical and political missions.

These missions often place the pilot thousands of miles from the nearest friendly recovery base, with only their intellect and the reliability of the U-2 to help them successfully complete the mission.

Flying the U-2 Dragon Lady is exciting and demanding; it is the most challenging aircraft to land in the United States' military arsenal. Prospective U-2 pilot applicants competitively chosen for the interview process must first pass a demanding three-sortie profile in the two-seat U-2 to determine their suitability. The acceptance rate for those applicants who are granted an interview runs about 50 percent.

Qualification training for the U-2 lasts five to seven months, depending on weather and airframe availability. This includes a checkout in the T-38, the companion trainer, as well as the chase car. The U-2 does not have conventional landing gear, just two single wheels mounted in its belly. Spring-loaded pogo wheels support the wings, and drop off on takeoff.

U-2 landings must be precise, and flown "to the knot." Every knot of speed over the planned landing speed puts the aircraft 1,000 feet farther down the runway. The pilot must balance the remaining fuel in each wing tank so the aircraft remains level when it lands. Because of the lack of depth perception from the cockpit,

A U-2 Dragon Lady can provide signals intelligence and real-time imagery. The U-2 still reigns supreme as the leader among manned intelligence, surveillance, and reconnaissance systems.

The U-2 Dragon Lady played often-indispensable roles from the Cuban Missile Crisis to Operation Iraqi Freedom. The chase car can be seen closing in on a landing U-2.

A KC-135 tanker on a taxiway while an NKC-135E takes off. The NKC-135E is a standard KC-135 Stratotanker that has been specially modified for the Air Force's Big Crow electronic warfare vulnerability assessment program. The airborne electronic warfare platform and its specialized ground elements make use of a wide variety of high-power antennas, modulators, and control systems to capture data to make detailed assessments of enemy vulnerability.

a chase car drives alongside the aircraft and calls the craft's speed as it touches down. When the airplane comes to a stop, the pogo wheels are reattached, and the pilot taxis to the ramp.

After graduation, a new U-2 pilot reports to the 99th Reconnaissance Squadron. The pilot typically spends about two months flying operational missions before rotating home for two months of continuation training. This cycle is repeated for about one-and-a-half years. This temporary duty (TDY) in the 1990s was as high as 240 days per year, due mainly to Operation Desert Storm, and ran about 180 days per year for newer line pilots until Operation Iraqi Freedom. After approximately three years in the U-2, pilots may be offered the opportunity to work as a formal training unit (FTU) IP, or they may request to return to their MWS.

TEST PILOTS

Test pilots have one of the most dangerous jobs in the Air Force. They train and work at the Air Force Flight Test Center at Edwards Air Force Base, California.

Pilots wishing to apply must have served at least 12 months as an AC in a major weapon system. Applicants must also be qualified instructor pilots in a major weapon system, or have at least 750 hours total time in that system.

It is through flight testing that test pilots will determine whether an aircraft will be suitable for its intended mission. The school teaches flight test techniques for evaluating aircraft performance, flying qualities, and systems characteristics. Test pilots not only test new fighter aircraft such as the F-22 Raptor, but also utility aircraft such as the CV-22 Osprey, an aircraft that flies like a cargo plane but takes off like a helicopter. They also assess new weapons systems, aircrew helmets, G-suits, stealth aircraft, heads-up displays, and other research programs. Contrary to the romantic notion of Hollywood films, test pilots do not have a cavalier attitude about flying. They follow carefully scripted flight profiles, and do not fly unscripted, dangerous aerial maneuvers. Natural ability in the air is necessary, of course, but a certain measured touch on the controls is needed to be a good test pilot.

Test pilot candidates are already some of the best pilots in the Air Force. The IP's attitude is different toward these candidates. It is not adversarial; it is more like a fellowship. They know within a year that the candidate is going to be a valuable asset to the test program.

Test pilot school offers pilots at least 140 flying hours in a 48-week course, about 200 hours less than most pilots fly in a year. Each candidate flies roughly 20 different aircraft while at the school, including a few rare and secret aircraft. After two years of test flying exper   , the pilot

continued on page 138

The Wright brothers were the first successful test pilots. In the 100 years of powered flight since the Wright Flyer, aircraft have evolved from wood-and-fabric contraptions into high-tech, supersonic designs that have touched the edge of space. A replica of the Wright brothers' Flyer takes off from Wright-Patterson Air Force Base.

Clouds of dust billow out behind a C-17 Globemaster III as it lands on a dry lakebed. Pilots are testing the performance of the Globemaster operating from a dirt airstrip.

The SR-71, unofficially known as the Blackbird, is an advanced long-range strategic-reconnaissance aircraft. The first flight of an SR-71 took place on December 22, 1964. The Air Force retired its fleet of SR-71s in January 1990, but returned some to active inventory in 1995, and began flying operational missions in January 1997. Throughout its 24-year career, the SR-71 remained the world's fastest and highest-flying operational aircraft.

The X-35 Joint Strike Fighter, currently in early test stages, is the stealth aircraft that will eventually replace the F-16.

During World War II, fighter pilots encountered a new and terrifying phenomenon. Rolling over into steep dives, they accelerated to speeds of 500 miles per hour and into the unknown region of transonic flight (Mach 0.7–1.3), where the effects of compressibility, loss of control, and devastating aerodynamic loads begin to take over, often with deadly results. The Bell X-1 rocket research plane (X for experimental) was the first in a series of rocket-powered research aircraft built for the Air Force and the National Advisory Committee on Aeronautics (NACA), the forerunner of NASA. The X-1 could not take off under its own power, but was attached in the bomb bay of a B-29 and dropped from altitude. Air Force Captain Chuck Yeager was the first man to break the sound barrier, on October 14, 1947, when the X-1 reached a speed of 700 miles per hour, or Mach 1.

The X-5 was the first aircraft capable of sweeping its wings for subsonic and transonic speeds. The swept-wing design improved the aircraft's performance as it approached the speed of sound. It bears a resemblance to the famous fighter of the Korean War, the F-86 Sabre Jet. This design led to the later swept-wing fighters.

The F-86 Sabre Jet was the Air Force's premier fighter during the Korean War. *Henry M. Holden*

An F-15E Strike Eagle is dropping wind-corrected munitions dispensers at Edwards Air Force Base. Before they are used in combat, new airborne munitions are tested at Edwards.

The director of the F-22 Raptor Combined Test Force program, Colonel Chris Seat, introduces retired Brigadier General Chuck Yeager to the F-22, the Air Force's next-generation combat aircraft.

Jackie Cochran is seen at the left with test pilot Chuck Yeager immediately after she became the first woman to break the sound barrier, in 1953.

An F-15 Eagle from the 416th Flight Test Squadron at Edwards Air Force Base, California, trails a B-1 bomber from the base's 419th FLTS.

Continued from page 132
may become part of the TPS staff. Some alumni become NASA astronauts.

ASTRONAUTS
Space is the final frontier for an Air Force pilot. One competitive pilot assignment is to the astronaut corps. At least 95 Air Force officers have earned astronaut wings, and at least 91 of them have been pilots. Pilots selected to be astronauts generally spend the rest of their careers with NASA.

Air Force pilots serve as space shuttle commanders, shuttle pilots, and mission specialists. The commander has onboard responsibility for the vehicle, the crew, and the success and safety of the mission. The pilot assists the commander in controlling and operating the craft.

Astronaut candidates are selected about every two years. Candidates require at least a bachelor's degree in engineering, biological science, physical science, or mathematics and at least 1,000 hours as AC in jet aircraft.

One of aviation's pioneering test pilots, Brigadier General Charles "Chuck" Yeager, although known for breaking the sound barrier in 1947, started flying as an enlisted member. In 1941, shortly after graduating from high school, he enlisted in the Army Air Corps and became an aircraft mechanic. Ironically, after throwing up during his first flight, he hated flying. A year later, to get away from kitchen duty, he jumped at the chance to become a "flying sergeant." He graduated flight training and flew in the European theater.

The CV-22 Osprey tiltrotor undergoing flight tests at Edwards Air Force Base.

The candidate must pass a NASA Class I space physical, similar to a military or civilian Class I flight physical, which includes meeting such vision standards as distance visual acuity of 20/70 or better, uncorrected, and near

Colonel Edwin E. "Buzz" Aldrin Jr., USAF (Ret.), was lunar module pilot for *Apollo 11,* July 16 to 24, 1969—the first manned lunar landing mission. He followed mission commander Neil Armstrong onto the lunar surface on July 20, 1969.

vision correctable to 20/20 for each eye; a blood pressure standard of 140/90 measured in a sitting position; and height between 64 and 76 inches.

Discipline panels evaluate applicants who meet the basic qualifications. Those selected as finalists are screened during a weeklong process of personal interviews, medical evaluations, and orientation. The Astronaut Selection Board's recommendations are based on the applicant's education, training, and experience, as well as unique qualifications and skills, such as being a geologist, physicist, or physician. There is a day of parachute training. Because several hundred applicants meet the requirements, the final selection is based largely on personal interviews. Astronauts must be team players, with just the right balance of individuality and self-reliance, and be

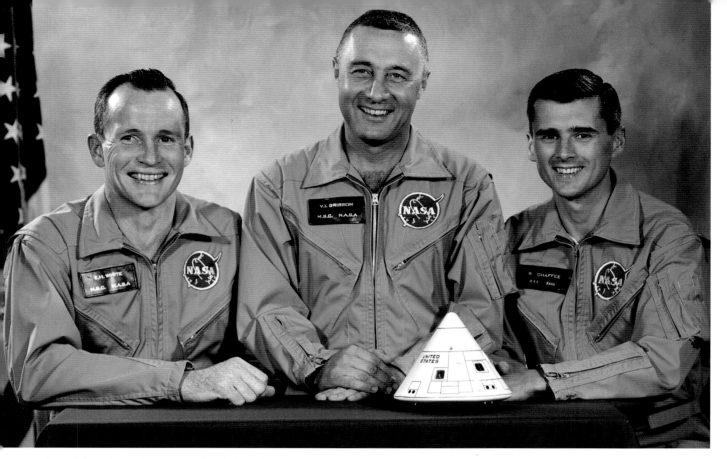

Shown left to right, Lieutenant Colonel Edward H. White II, USAF; Lieutenant Colonel Virgil I. Grissom, USAF; and Lieutenant Commander Roger Chaffee, USN, were lost in the *Apollo I* capsule fire on the ground in 1967. Grissom was the first Air Force officer and the second American in space, in 1961. White was the first American to step outside a spacecraft and let go, setting him adrift in the zero gravity of space for 23 minutes. *NASA*

Even though an Air Force pilot has spent several years in various flight schools and in operational units, it will take another year or two of training to become an astronaut. Training and missions are so rigorous that pilots quickly realize how dangerous it can be. *Apollo 12* (seen here) successfully returned to Earth. However, *Apollo 1* never made it off the launch pad. *Henry M. Holden*

Payload specialist Lieutenant Colonel Michael Anderson and spacecraft commander Colonel Rick D. Husband were both lost in the Columbia accident in 2003. Husband was a test pilot and veteran of one space flight. This was Anderson's second space flight. NASA

An Air Force pilot was lost on each of two space shuttle mission accidents: Major Francis R. Scobee and Lieutenant Colonel Ellison S. Onizuka. Scobee had joined the Air Force as an enlisted person, went to night school, and in 1965 completed a B.S. degree in aerospace engineering. This made it possible for Scobee to receive an officer's commission and enter the Air Force pilot training program. He was the shuttle commander on *Challenger*.

After receiving his commission at the University of Colorado through the four-year ROTC program as a distinguished military graduate, Onizuka entered on active duty with the Air Force in January 1970. He attended the USAF Test Pilot School in August 1974. He later served as chief of the engineering support section in the training resources branch. He first flew as a mission specialist on STS 51-C, the first Space Shuttle Department of Defense mission, and was also mission specialist on STS 51-L.

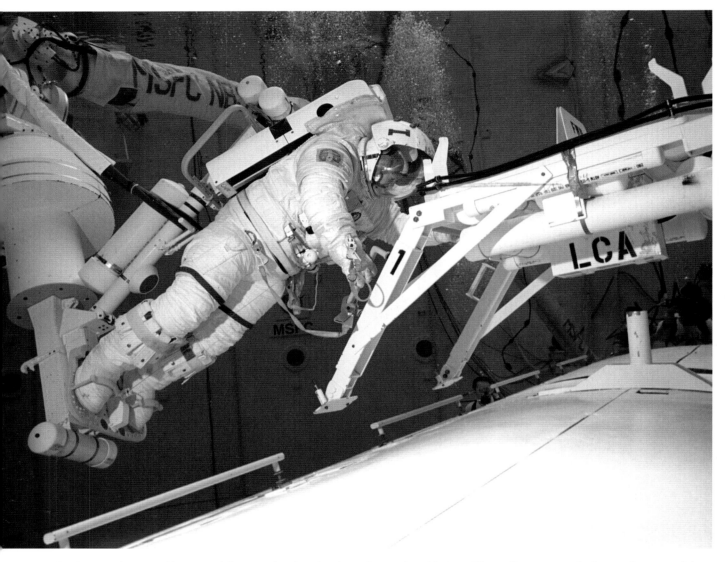

NASA also uses the neutral buoyancy laboratory (NBL) to simulate microgravity. This 6.4-million-gallon water tank allows trainees to safely practice their movements as though in near-zero gravity. Air Force pilot and astronaut Susan J. Helms is in the NBL wearing a pressure spacesuit adapted for the water. She will be made neutrally buoyant by attaching floats and weights to her suit until she neither rises nor falls in the tank. *NASA*

highly skilled in several technical areas in order to be effective crewmembers.

The training is physically and mentally challenging. Although the pilot has already experienced some of the training, they will now experience it again. The training includes being dragged behind a motorboat, parachuting through trees, scuba diving in cold water, and being lifted by helicopter from a bobbing raft in the ocean. These skills are necessary in case the crew has to bail out of the shuttle or make an emergency landing.

In space there are also physical and mental challenges. In the absence of gravity, muscles (including the heart) weaken. Astronauts must be in excellent physical condition to endure both the training and the mission.

MICROGRAVITY
Using a modified KC-135 aircraft, all astronaut candidates undergo simulated microgravity to prepare for the real thing in space. Even though they may be pilots who have experienced G forces, they still need to experience

On July 23, 1999, Colonel Eileen Collins became the first woman to command the $2 billion space shuttle *Columbia*. At the time of her flight, Collins was one of only 27 American women who had flown into space. She earned her Air Force commission through ROTC and graduated from flight training in 1979. Collins flew C-141 cargo jets and spent two years as a C-141 aircraft commander. In 1986, she became an assistant professor of mathematics at the Air Force Academy, where she was also an IP.

extended periods of negative Gs (or microgravity) in a jet nicknamed the "vomit comet." The airplane climbs to about 36,000 feet and then dives toward earth in a large, parabolic arc. The pilot flies these arcs by pulling the nose up to a 45-degree angle until the wings no longer have lift. At the top of arc the trainees experiences more than 2 Gs. Over the top of the arc the pilot pushes the stick forward, and continues to pitch over until the airplane is 45 degrees nose down, creating negative Gs.

Challenger, mated to a specially modified B-747 jet, approaches the Kennedy Space Center at Cape Canaveral, Florida. Mechanical and human failures caused *Challenger* to explode on launch. Investigators ruled that a faulty O-ring seal on the right solid-rocket booster caused the explosion. *NASA*

New astronauts also need to train in the shuttle before they are assigned to an actual flight. At the Shuttle Avionics Integration Laboratory (SAIL), the spacecraft commander and pilot learn each of the systems. As with any aircraft, the systems must be memorized and their functions understood. If there is an in-flight emergency, the commander and pilot will not have to think about what to do; they will react with the correct response immediately.

The spacecraft commander and the pilot will practice landing the shuttle in the shuttle training aircraft (STA). The STA is a modified Grumman American Aviation-built Gulfstream II executive jet, modified to simulate an orbiter's cockpit, motion, visual cues, and handling characteristics. The STA will duplicate the orbiter's descent trajectory from approximately 35,000 feet AGL to landing on the runway. The orbiter touchdown speed is 213 to 226 miles per hour, and the pilots duplicate this profile in the STA. The orbiters are unpowered during re-entry, so their high-speed glide must be perfectly

Columbia, seen here on its last liftoff, was destroyed on reentry because of a breach in the left wing caused by a piece of foam insulation that fell from the shuttle's external tank during launch. *NASA*

Susan Helms became the first U.S. military woman in space in 1993 and the first woman to inhabit the International Space Station in 2001. She is co-holder of the world record—with crewmate Army Colonel Jim Voss—for the longest space walk, 8 hours and 56 minutes. Helms, who graduated from the Air Force Academy in 1980, completed Air Force Test Pilot School at Edwards Air Force Base, California, in 1987. After a 12-year NASA career that included 211 days in space, Lieutenant Colonel Helms returned to the Air Force in July 2002 to take a position as the chief of the Space Control Division of the Requirements Directorate of Air Force Space Command. A veteran of five space flights, Helms logged 5,064 hours in space. *NASA*

executed the first time. They have no go-around or missed approach capability.

Training continues even after astronauts have a flight assignment. About 10 weeks before the liftoff, the astronauts begin to simulate the mission with the Mission Control team. These simulations permit the crew and Mission Control to practice operating as a team.

PREDATOR PILOTS

Indian Springs Auxiliary Field (Nellis Air Force Base) is home of the Predator unmanned aerial vehicle (UAV), the latest challenging pilot assignment. One pilot and two enlisted sensor operators make up the crew of a Predator aircraft. The Predator's pilot operates the aircraft by remote control from a state-of-the-art ground-control station, miles away from the battlefield. They are responsible for dropping weapons, and must have the same qualifications as any other pilot or forward air controller (FAC). The sensor operators control the cameras and radar.

The Predator has a single rear-mounted (pusher) propeller, with a four-cylinder engine. It has a 48-foot, 7-inch wingspan and is 27 feet long. It carries 665 pounds (about 100 gallons) of fuel and can fly a 500-nautical-mile radius at altitudes up to 25,000 feet. The Predator can remain on-station in excess of 24 hours—five times longer on a target than the manned U-2 reconnaissance plane. Each Predator aircraft can be disassembled into six main components and loaded into a container nicknamed "the coffin." This enables all system components and support equipment to be rapidly deployed worldwide. The largest component, the ground control station, can be transported in a C-130.

Sitting at the controls, a pilot of the 31st Test and Evaluation Squadron, Edwards Air Force Base, California, monitors the RQ-4A Global Hawk from inside the Mission Control Element (MCE). The MCE is responsible for key mission plan elements, including aircraft and mission payload control and flight, communication, and sensor processing. Unlike smaller UAVs such as the Predator, which are "flown" from a ground station by a pilot using a joystick and watching real-time images provided by nose-mounted cameras, the Global Hawk is an autonomous vehicle whose entire mission is pre-planned and controlled by a computer. Currently, the U-2 sensor payload is 4,700 pounds, compared to 1,800 pounds for the Global Hawk.

The Predator ground station is like a large laptop flight simulator with two screens. The upper 20-inch screen has a map of the target area with a symbol of the aircraft superimposed. The pilot must keep the Predator within a certain corridor a few miles wide, which is also displayed on the map. Once the pilot levels off at altitude, they can engage the autopilot to hold altitude, heading, and airspeed.

Pilots fly the Predator aircraft like any other aircraft, complying with headings, altitudes, and airspeeds as directed by ATC. Instead of looking through a cockpit windshield, the pilot is watching a 30-degree field of vision from the aircraft's nose camera. Part of the challenge is flying the Predator at 80 miles per hour with a narrow field of vision. The pilot has no depth perception and has to remember what camera they are looking through, since several are at their disposal. The daylight camera, located in the aircraft's nose, is used for flight control, while others are used for surveillance in low-light environments such as smoke, clouds, or haze. The Predator's infrared eye pierces the night, capturing the landscape with shades of white, black, and gray.

The lower screen reports the transponder code, airspeed, angle of attack, altitude, and other information, such as engine manifold pressure. Two smaller screens show variable-information tables, displaying the positions of the flaps, for example, and engine temperature.

The Predator uses electro-optic, infrared, and synthetic-aperture radar sensors to transmit images in real time via satellite link to ground-control stations, or to a lurking, or loitering, strike aircraft, such as an AC-130 Gunship, waiting to be vectored to a ground target. Predators provide ground commanders below with up-to-the-second, real-time battlefield information. Having a remote FAC aircraft provides the flexibility needed for missions previously reserved for manned aircraft. Predator pilots are able to scout ahead, report on enemy positions around a bend in the road, or over a hill, without putting a human pilot in harm's way. In the Vietnam War, for example, at least 219 FACs were lost in combat.

The Predator has evolved from a purely intelligence-oriented reconnaissance vehicle. It can find the enemy and get a fix on its position, destroy stationary and mobile targets with Hellfire missiles, and do bomb damage assessment (BDA) immediately after the strike.

The Predator may also be used to locate targets for waiting strike aircraft. The Predator's pilot provides the attack aircraft with run-in and egress headings, target information, altitude, and geographic deconfliction (i.e., determining if there is a potential conflict, such as an air strike, with friendly forces in the area). After a strike, Predators can provide instant BDA, allowing for immediate follow-up strikes, if necessary.

AIR FORCE ONE
The mission of Air Force One is to provide air transportation for the President of the United States. Only Air Force pilots are allowed to fly this airplane, and even the pilots need special permission to go aboard the aircraft. In 1944, Franklin Delano Roosevelt became the first American president to travel by air, and for the next 20 years various types of four-engine, propeller-driven aircraft were used for presidential air travel. In 1962, the first jet aircraft, a Boeing 707, was used as Air Force One. In 1990, the 707 was replaced by the Boeing 747-200.

AIR FORCE TWO
Air Force Two is the name given to the Air Force aircraft in which the Vice President travels. Anne Fletcher is a retired former pilot of Air Force Two. She graduated with the first U.S. Air Force Academy class to include women in 1980. Within three years, she became an AC in a C-141. By April 1991, Fletcher had 2,800 flying hours, and was an IP. "A fellow C-12 IP decided she did not want to fly the C-137 [Air Force Two]," said Fletcher, who by this time had been promoted to major. So Fletcher took over her training slot.

At this point, women had not been completely accepted by some of the male pilots, so Fletcher had to be on guard for mischief makers. In one incident, her crew "forgot" her at a hotel. Eager to please, she had shown up fifteen minutes early for the bus to the airport. Fletcher had already eaten, but the rest of the crew decided to eat breakfast at the bus departure time. After she had sat for 45 minutes drinking coffee . . . and more coffee, the crew showed no sign of movement, so she dashed to the restroom. When she returned five minutes later, the entire crew and the buses were gone. Not to be thwarted so easily, Fletcher grabbed a taxi to the airport. "The crew was astounded when I walked up to the airplane about the same time they 'realized' I was missing. Several weeks later, I overheard some flight stewards retelling the story at the expense of my fellow pilots. They said, 'She got the perfect revenge! She calmly reminded the pilots that it was "her leg," and proceeded to fly and make the smoothest

The current presidential fleet consists of two specially configured Boeing 747-200 series aircraft—tail numbers 28000 and 29000—with the Air Force designation VC-25A. When the president is aboard either aircraft, or any Air Force aircraft, the radio call sign is "Air Force One." When the first lady travels alone on the airplane, it uses its tail number as its call sign. The call sign Air Force One was first used in 1959 after the president's airplane came close to having a midair collision with a commercial airliner with the same I.D. number.

These VC-25As are flown by the presidential aircrew and are part of the Air Mobility Command's 89th Airlift Wing, based at Andrews Air Force Base, Maryland. To be an Air Force One pilot, one must have more than 2,000 flying hours, worldwide flight experience, and a spotless record. The 26 crewmembers are carefully screened Air Force personnel with exemplary service histories.

The VC-25A (V for Very Important Person) can fly 9,600 miles without refueling and can accommodate up to 70 passengers. It contains a presidential suite/stateroom, executive dressing room/shower, a presidential office, and a medical treatment room. It has almost as much communications equipment as the White House, with 84 telephones, including 28 that are secure and encrypted, 57 antennas, 19 television monitors, 11 videocassette players, and several computers. There are over 238 miles of electrical wiring, more than twice the amount in a normal 747.

landing I've ever felt.'" But as typically happens, her new reputation failed to convince some diehards.

"I had flown in the jumpseat for Vice President Quayle," Fletcher recalls, "and I finally had a chance to make the landing for Vice President Gore in April of 1993. I was a master at landing the C-137, but I fear Mr. Gore may never want another woman pilot. Knowing I was about to be reassigned, and that this would be my only chance to fly for such a high-ranking person, I decided to enjoy the moment. This was not a good choice.

"It was a flight from Atlanta to D.C., a short flight, and like many approaches with vice presidents, we were trying to make up time. We flew at 250 knots until about 10 miles out, then barely slowed to maximum, gear-lowering speed by the final approach fix. I kept the speed up until the short final. Ordinarily, this was no problem. We practiced fast approaches, and flew with two navigators who monitored our speed, time, and position. Alas, instead of concentrating on my flare, I thought, I'm flying the second most powerful person in the free world. Although it was a safe landing, I made what the 89th

A view beneath the Thunderbirds F-16s in formation. The Thunderbirds squadron is an Air Combat Command unit composed of eight pilots (including six demonstration pilots), four support officers, three civilians, and about 130 enlisted personnel. The F-16 Fighting Falcon represents the full range of capabilities possessed by the Air Force's tactical fighters. This highly maneuverable multi-role fighter has proven itself to be one of the world's best precision tactical bombers and air-to-air combat aircraft. The only modifications needed to prepare the aircraft for its air-demonstration role are installing a smoke-generating system in the space normally reserved for the 20mm cannon and painting the aircraft in Thunderbird colors.

classifies as a 'carrier landing.' To their credit, my peers didn't say a word."

U.S. AIR FORCE THUNDERBIRDS

The Thunderbirds are called America's "Ambassadors in Blue." They represent the United States and its armed forces, and project international goodwill. The Thunderbirds perform precision formation and solo flying routines in six F-16 Fighting Falcons at air shows every year. The demonstration season lasts from March to November, with the winter months used for training at Nellis Air Force Base, Nevada. The team begins the training season with full practice sessions four times a week. After the first of the year, the sessions become two a day. Every maneuver in every practice session is evaluated, rated, and debriefed after every session.

Competition to be a Thunderbird pilot is intense. The commander/leader flies the Number One jet, leading all air demonstrations, and commands the 130-person squadron. The commander must be a lieutenant colonel or lieutenant colonel select, have a minimum of 1,000 hours flight time as a first pilot/instructor in a jet fighter or trainer aircraft, and be currently or previously qualified in a fighter aircraft.

The demonstration pilots, usually captains or majors, must have a minimum of 1,000 hours of flight time as a first pilot/instructor in a jet fighter or trainer aircraft, and be currently or previously qualified in a fighter aircraft. These pilots must also not have more than 12 years of active commissioned service at the time they apply.

Recently, after careful screening and interviewing hundreds of applicants, 52 became semifinalists. That was narrowed down to nine finalists, for two open slots.

The Thunderbirds' performance demonstrates the capabilities of the pilots and the F-16 Fighting Falcon.

The Thunderbirds squadron performs no more than 88 air demonstrations each year and has never canceled a performance due to maintenance problems.

In the team maneuvers, the pilots routinely pull 4 Gs. In the solo maneuvers, the pilots pull up to 9 Gs. The pilots perform approximately 30 maneuvers in the 75-minute demonstration.

The flight leader makes the call, "Thunderbirds let's run 'em up," and their takeoff roll begins. The four-ship formation, powered by more than 100,000 pounds of thrust from four Pratt & Whitney engines, thunders down the runway. As the planes lift-off and begin their climb, the slot pilot quickly edges their aircraft from the right wing tightly into position to form the signature Thunderbird Diamond.

Following the Diamond, the lead solo clears the runway, and snaps an immediate 360-degree aileron roll. Finally, the opposing solo powers their aircraft nearly straight up. Reversing direction, they fly back past the crowd—all within the length of the runway—in a maneuver called the Split-S.

Thunderbird 5 maneuvers in front of the crowd flying in a high-speed inverted pass. Thunderbird 6, also

Thunderbird Two concentrates on maintaining his left-wing position. Pilots in diamond formation must overcome the natural tendency to look at the ground, and instead devote full attention to the lead aircraft.

Thunderbirds refueling.

inverted, rolls in from the opposite direction. One rolls 360 degrees right at show center, with the inverted-to-inverted pass.

Thunderbird 6 conducts four maximum-performance aileron rolls four times in just six seconds. Later, screaming overhead at Mach 0.98, Thunderbird 6 performs the Thunderbird Sneak Pass, a classic example of tactical surprise. Using speed and agility in maneuvers like this allows Air Force pilots to reach their target undetected, hit it hard, and return to fight another day.

In air combat, if you cannot turn tight, you cannot fight. The F-16 Fighting Falcon can do both. One Thunderbird performs a full-afterburner high-performance turn directly in front of the crowd.

CROSS INTO THE BLUE

The September 11, 2001, terrorist attacks forever changed the United States and ushered in its policy of pre-emptive strikes. Operation Enduring Freedom in Afghanistan was the first use of this concept. It proved that cooperation between air power and special operations forces could produce a swift victory against unconventional forces, with less collateral damage than in previous wars.

Operation Iraqi Freedom in early 2003 was the best-covered war in history. During the 24-hour-a-day coverage by imbedded news media, live images of U.S. armored columns racing to Baghdad stole the spotlight. What TV viewers did not see in such up-close detail was the merciless

An F-16 from Tyndall Air Force Base, Florida, takes off.

Several years ago, icing was suspected in the crash of a civilian ATR-72 commuter turboprop airliner. Subsequently, an Edwards Air Force Base KC-135A icing tanker performed icing tests on a similar aircraft.

An F-15 Eagle pilot from the Florida Air National Guard's 125th Fighter Wing in Jacksonville flies a combat air patrol mission above the NASA vehicle-assembly building at Cape Canaveral, Florida.

pounding from the sky by U.S. fighters and bombers that was critical to victory over the Iraqi military.

Off-screen, the Air Force led a massive air campaign using joint directed attack munitions (JDAMS), precision-guided bombs that made it possible for troops and tanks on the ground to roll into the capital with unprecedented speed. U.S. Air Force pilots led the way flying the most missions, dropping the most bombs, and using the most aircraft. Aerial strikes wiped out entire enemy divisions, or pummeled them to the point that they were no longer cohesive units by the time ground forces arrived.

A new method of close-air support got its first true combat test in Iraq. The technique called for "racked-and-stacked" fighters, bombers, tankers, and reconnaissance aircraft to fly in "racetrack" patterns over Baghdad, where they were in position to respond instantly to air-support requests from ground forces.

Three B-2 Spirits in the night sky.

When the chips are down, the Air Force goes in first. The Air Mobility Command is ready on a moment's notice to transport personnel and equipment anywhere in the world. Without Air Force pilots and their support personnel, the other services would not be able to get to their destination as fast as they do.

Over the past century, aircraft have evolved from rickety, boxkite-like airplanes into supersonic ghosts seemingly immune to mortal weapons. Thanks to the cadre of highly motivated, highly skilled, and dedicated men and women of the United States Air Force, the United States enters the uncertain landscape of the twenty-first century with the most powerful, swiftest, and most flexible military force the world has ever seen.

153

Appendix 1

Twentieth Century Air Force Aces

To become an ace, a pilot must be credited with five air-to-air victories, known as kills. In the lists below, the number of confirmed kills follows each name.

Top 20 U.S. World War I aces (out of 70 total U.S. aces in WWI)*

Captain Edward V. Rickenbacker, 26
Second Lieutenant Frank Luke Jr., 18
First Lieutenant George A. Vaughn Jr., 13
First Lieutenant Field E. Kindley, 12
First Lieutenant Elliot W. Springs, 12
First Lieutenant Reed G. Landis, 10
First Lieutenant Jacques M. Swaab, 10
First Lieutenant Paul P. Baer, 9
First Lieutenant Thomas G. Cassady, 9
First Lieutenant Lloyd A. Hamilton, 9
First Lieutenant Chester E. Wright, 9
First Lieutenant Henry R. Clay Jr., 8
Captain Hamilton Coolidge, 8
Second Lieutenant John O. Donaldson, 8
First Lieutenant William P. Erwin, 8
First Lieutenant Frank O. Hunter, 8
Second Lieutenant Clinton S. Jones, 8
Captain James A. Meissner, 8
First Lieutenant Martinus Stenseth, 8
Second Lieutenant Wilbert W. White Jr., 8

In World War I, many American pilots flew with Allied services instead of the U.S. military and are not included in this list.

Top 17 Army Air Forces World War II aces (out of 701 total Army Air Forces aces)

Major Richard I. Bong, 40
Major Thomas B. McGuire Jr., 38
Lieutenant Colonel Francis S. Gabreski, 28 (plus 6.5 in Korea)
Captain Robert S. Johnson, 27
Colonel Charles H. MacDonald, 27
Major George E. Preddy Jr., 26.83
Lieutenant Colonel John C. Meyer, 24

Colonel David C. Schilling, 22.5
Lieutenant Colonel Gerald R. Johnson, 22
Colonel Neel E. Kearby, 22
Major Jay T. Robbins, 22
Captain Fred J. Christensen, 21.5
Captain Ray S. Wetmore, 21.25
Captain John J. Voll, 21
Major Walker M. Mahurin, 20.75 (plus 3.5 in Korea)
Lieutenant Colonel Thomas J. Lynch, 20
Lieutenant Colonel Robert B. Westbrook, 20

Top 11 Air Force Korean War aces (38 total U.S. Air Force aces)

Captain Joseph C. McConnell Jr., 16
Major James Jabara, 15 (plus 1.5 in World War II)
Captain Manuel J. Fernandez, 14.5
Major George A. Davis Jr., 14 (plus 7 in World War II)
Colonel Royal N. Baker, 13 (plus 3.5 in World War II)
Major Fredrick C. Blesse, 10
Captain Harold E. Fischer, 10
Lieutenant Colonel Vermont Garrison, 10 (plus 7.33 in World War II)
Captain Lonnie R. Moore, 10
Captain Ralph S. Parr Jr., 10
Colonel James K. Johnson, 10

Air Force Aces of the Vietnam War (3 total)

Captain Charles DeBellevue**, 6
Captain Jeffrey S. Feinstein**, 5
Captain R. Stephen Ritchie, 5

**Weapons systems officer ace*

Aces of two wars

Six aces from World War II went on to become aces during the Korean War.
Colonel Harrison R. Thyng, 8 in World War II, 7 in Korea
Lieutenant Colonel Francis S. Gabreski, 28 in World War II, 6.5 in Korea
Lieutenant Colonel Vermont Garrison, 7.33 in World War II, 10 in Korea
Major George A. Davis Jr., 7 in World War II, 14 in Korea
Major James P. Hagerstrom, 6 in World War II, 8.5 in Korea
Major William T. Whisner, 15.5 in World War II, 5.5 in Korea

Appendix 2

Records Achieved by U.S. Air Force Pilots

September 18, 1947 The U.S. Air Force is established as a separate service.

October 14, 1947 Captain Charles E. Yeager makes the first supersonic flight in the rocket-powered Bell XS-I (later redesigned X-1) over Muroc Dry Lake, California.

October 21, 1947 The first flight of the Northrop YB-49 flying-wing jet bomber is made. The Air Force's Northrop B-2 Stealth bomber bears a family resemblance to this plane.

June 26, 1948 Operation Vittles, the Berlin Airlift, begins with Douglas C-47 crews bringing 80 tons of supplies into the city on the first day. By the time it ends on September 30, 1949, the airlift will have delivered a total of 2,324,257 tons of food, fuel, and supplies to the beleaguered city.

July 1, 1949 The Air Force becomes the first service to announce an end to racial segregation in its ranks.

November 8, 1950 First Lieutenant Russell J. Brown, flying an Air Force F-80 Shooting Star, downs a North Korean MiG-15 in the first battle between jet aircraft.

November 30, 1951 Major George A. Davis Jr. becomes the first USAF ace of two wars; he has a total of seven confirmed kills in World War II and 14 in Korea.

May 20, 1951 Captain James Jabara becomes the Air Force's first jet-versus-jet ace. He eventually downs 15 enemy planes in Korea.

September 1, 1953 The first jet-to-jet air refueling takes place between a USAF Boeing KB-47 and a "standard" B-47.

April 1, 1954 President Dwight D. Eisenhower signs into law a bill creating the Air Force Academy.

December 10, 1954 To determine if a pilot can eject from an airplane at supersonic speed and live, Lieutenant Colonel John Paul Stapp, a flight surgeon, rides a rocket sled to 632 miles per hour, decelerates to zero in 125 seconds, and survives more than 35 times the force of gravity. This experiment was conducted at a test track at Holloman Air Force Base, New Mexico.

July 11, 1955 The first class (306 cadets) is sworn in at the Air Force Academy's temporary location at Lowry Air Force Base, Colorado.

August 16, 1960 Captain Joseph Kittinger completes the world's highest skydive: a 19.5-mile leap to earth. The record still stands today. He freefell at speeds of up to 714 miles per hour, approaching the speed of sound without the protection of an aircraft or space vehicle and experiencing temperatures as low as –94 degrees Fahrenheit. He was in freefall for 4.5 minutes before he opened his parachute at 18,000 feet.

July 21, 1961 Captain Virgil I. "Gus" Grissom becomes the first Air Force astronaut off the ground, flying a suborbital flight to 118 miles above the earth aboard the *Liberty Bell 7* capsule.

July 17, 1962 Major Robert M. White, flying a North American X-15, number three research aircraft from Edwards Air Force Base, sets a world record in altitude in an aircraft launched from a carrier airplane, 314,750 feet.

March 23, 1965 Air Force Major Virgil I. "Gus" Grissom becomes the first astronaut in the manned space-flight program to go aloft a second time, as he and navy Lieutenant Commander John W. Young are launched in *Gemini 3* on the first Gemini mission.

January 2, 1967 Colonel Robin Olds becomes the first (and only) U.S. Air Force ace with victories in World War II and Vietnam (12 in World War II and 4 in Vietnam).

July 16, 1971 Jeanne M. Holm becomes the first female general officer in the Air Force.

July 26, 1971 A *Saturn V* launch vehicle lifted off its launch pad at Kennedy Space Center, Florida, carrying the *Apollo 15* spacecraft. Aboard the command module were commander Colonel David R. Scott, lunar module pilot Lieutenant Colonel James B. Irwin, and command module pilot Major Alfred M. Worden Jr.—the first all-Air Force Apollo crew.

August 28, 1972 Captain Richard S. Ritchie, flying an F-4 Phantom, with his back-seater, Captain Charles B. DeBellevue, shoots down his fifth MiG-21 near Hanoi, becoming the Air Force's first ace since the Korean War.

September 1, 1974 Majors James V. Sullivan and Noel Widdifield set a New York-to-London speed record of 1,806.964 miles per hour in a Lockheed SR-71A. The trip takes 1 hour, 54 minutes, and 55 seconds.

September 1, 1975 General Daniel "Chappie" James Jr. becomes the first African-American officer to achieve four-star rank in the U.S. military.

July 28, 1976 SR-71 pilots Major Adolphus H. Bledsoe, Captain Robert C. Helt, and Captain Eldon W. Joersz set three world flight records over Beale Air Force Base, California: altitude in horizontal flight, 85,068.997 feet; speed over a straight course, 2,193.16 miles per hour; and speed over a closed course, 2,092.294 miles per hour.

May 28, 1980 The Air Force Academy graduates its first female cadets. Ninety-seven women are commissioned as second lieutenants. Lieutenant Kathleen Conly graduates eighth in her class.

June 10, 1982 Strategic Air Command's first all-female crew performs a five-hour training mission that includes a mid-air refueling of a B-52 Stratofortress aircraft.

September 24, 1987 The Air Force Thunderbirds fly for a crowd of 5,000 in Beijing. It has been nearly 40 years since a U.S. combat aircraft flew over and landed on Chinese soil.

November 10, 1988 The Air Force reveals the existence of the Lockheed F-117A Stealth fighter, operational since 1983.

June 10, 1989 Captain Jacquelyn S. Parker becomes the first female pilot to graduate from the Air Force Test Pilot School at Edwards Air Force Base, California.

January 17, 1991 B-52G crews from the Second Bomb Wing, Barksdale Air Force Base, Louisiana, takeoff to begin what will become the longest bombing mission in history. Carrying 39 AGM-86C air-launched cruise missiles, the bomber crews fly to the Middle East and launch their missiles against high-priority targets in Iraq, a 35-hour, nonstop, roundtrip combat mission.

April 28, 1993 Defense Secretary Les Aspin removes the Defense Department's restrictions on female participation in aerial combat.

December 2, 1993 Air Force Colonel Richard O. Covey, pilot and mission commander, pilots the fifth flight of the shuttle *Endeavour*, which sets a record for the greatest number of spacewalks—five. On the same flight, Air Force Lieutenant Colonel Tom Akers becomes the U.S. record holder for cumulative spacewalk time, with 29 hours and 40 minutes.

July 23, 1994 Retired Lieutenant General Benjamin Davis Jr. the first African-American Air Force general and founder of the Tuskegee Airman, is inducted into the National Aviation Hall of Fame in Dayton, Ohio.

February 3, 1995 Lieutenant Colonel Eileen Collins becomes the first woman to pilot a space shuttle.

March 2, 1995 The U.S. space shuttle *Endeavour*, piloted by USAF Lieutenant Colonel William G. Gregory, sets the record for the longest U.S. shuttle flight, besting shuttle *Columbia*'s previous endurance record by more than 45 hours.

September 25, 1995 Second Lieutenant Kelly Flinn graduates as the Air Force's first female B-52 bomber pilot.

May 5, 1996 Major General Betty L. Mullis becomes the first female to head an Air Force flying wing, the 940th Air Refueling Wing. At the time, Mullis is a command pilot with 4,900 hours.

Appendix 3

Medal of Honor Recipients: Air Force Pilots

Over the history of the Air Force, 51 pilots distinguished themselves for "conspicuous gallantry and intrepidity, above and beyond the call of duty."

World War I (4 awarded, 3 posthumously (P))
First Lieutenant Harold Ernest Goettler 1918 (P)
First Lieutenant Edward Vernon Rickenbacker 1918
Second Lieutenant Erwin Russell Bleckley 1918 (P)
Second Lieutenant Frank Luke Jr. 1918 (P)

Peacetime awards
General William Mitchell 1946 (P)
Captain Charles A. Lindbergh Jr. 1928
    (Special Act of Congress)

World War II (28 awarded, 15 posthumously)
1942 (3 awarded, 2 posthumously)
Brigadier General James H. Doolittle
Colonel Demas Thurlow Craw (P)
Captain Harl Pease Jr. (P)

1943 (11 awarded, 5 posthumously)
Brigadier General Kenneth Newton Walker (P)
Colonel Leon William Johnson
Colonel John Riley Kane
Colonel Neel Ernest Kearby
Lieutenant Colonel Addison Earl Baker (P)
Major Ralph Cheli (P)
Major John Louis Jerstad (P)
Major Raymond Harrell Wilkins
Major Jay Zeamer Jr.
Second Lieutenant Lloyd Herbert Hughes (P)
Second Lieutenant John Cary Morgan

1944 (12 awarded, 8 posthumously)
Brigadier General Frederick Walker Castle (P)
Lieutenant Colonel James Howell Howard
Lieutenant Colonel Leon R. Vance Jr. (P)
Major Richard Ira Bong
Major Horace Seaver Carswell Jr. (P)

Major Thomas B. McGuire (P)
Captain Darrell Robins Lindsey (P)
First Lieutenant Donald J. Gott (P)
First Lieutenant William Robert Lawley Jr.
First Lieutenant Edward Stanley Michael
First Lieutenant Donald Dale Pucket (P)
Second Lieutenant William E. Metzger Jr. (P)

1945 (2 awarded, 1 posthumously)
Major William A. Shomo
First Lieutenant Raymond L. Knight (P)

Korean War (4 awarded, 4 posthumously)
Major George A. Davis Jr. 1952 (P)
Major Charles J. Loring Jr. 1952 (P)
Major Louis J. Sebille 1950 (P)
Captain John S. Walmsley Jr. 1951 (P)

Vietnam War (11 awarded, 3 posthumously)
Colonel George E. Day 1967
Colonel William A. Jones III 1968
Lieutenant Colonel Joe M. Jackson 1968
Lieutenant Colonel Leo Thorsness 1967
Major Merlyn Hans Dethlefsen 1967
Major Bernard F. Fisher 1966
Captain Steven L. Bennett 1972 (P)
Captain James Philip Fleming 1968
Captain Lance Peter Sijan 1967 (P)
Captain Hilliard Almond Wilbanks 1967 (P)
Captain Gerald Orren Young 1967

(Verified by William T. Y'Blood, Chief, Reference Branch Air Force History)

Index

159

**To Be a
U.S. Army Ranger**
ISBN: 0-7603-1314-8

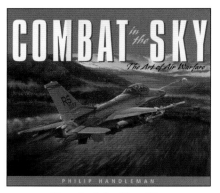

Combat in the Sky
ISBN: 0-7603-1468-3

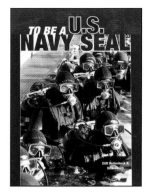

**To Be a
U.S. Navy SEAL**
ISBN: 0-7603-1404-7

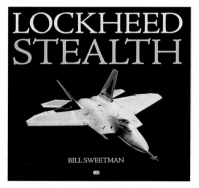

Lockheed Stealth
ISBN: 0-7603-0852-7

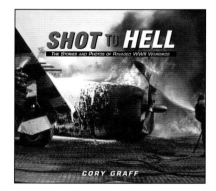

Shot to Hell
ISBN: 0-7603-1609-0

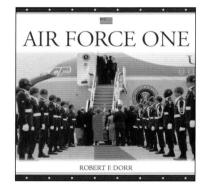

Air Force One
ISBN: 0-7603-1055-6

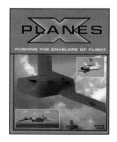

X-Planes
ISBN: 0-7603-1584-1

**U.S. Air Force
Special Ops**
ISBN: 0-7603-0733-4

Black Hawk
ISBN: 0-7603-1591-4